CW00864408

IN SEARCH
OF SOMETHING

DAVE BRIESMEISTER

authorHOUSE®

AuthorHouse™
1663 Liberty Drive
Bloomington, IN 47403
www.authorhouse.com
Phone: 1-800-839-8640

First published by AuthorHouse 9/24/2010

ISBN: 978-1-4520-8398-8 (sc)
ISBN: 978-1-4520-8399-5 (e)

Library of Congress Control Number: 2010914364

Printed in the United States of America

This book is printed on acid-free paper.

Chapter One

It was a clear dark night. The snow cracked beneath our feet and the ropes creaked with the frost as men swore quietly in the frigid darkness. People moved equipment around, had quiet conversations, some complained about being tired before the fun even had begun. One of the guys said "I've got to piss" and moved off into the darkness for a minute.

Slowly, the leaders of the expedition got some sense of order to the mess of ropes, equipment, people. Selections were made; decisions taken about who should do what, what should go where. Some articles of a non essential nature were eliminated from packs and bags. Everyone wanted to be under way, yet no one wanted to leave the perceived security of the camp, for the unknown and uncertain day ahead.

Orders were issued, voices became stronger, men began to form teams and string them out. I had been selected for the lead position in the fourth team back from the front. I was not told why and I did not question it. Later, as the black morning began to give way to the crack of dawn, I came to know the full measure of what leader meant. The man in the rope behind me could not, would not, keep pace. I found myself pulling another person, the lazy bastard, up through the snow, hour after hour, into the glacier area. There we slowed the pace as crampons were laced on to our boots, men stopped to piss; snack bars were eaten on the march, etc. My lazy bastard never did pick it up. I pulled, dragged, swore and sweated that SOB all the way, all night and into the day, up the mountain. Had the choice been mine, I'd have dumped him in the first crevasse we encountered on the way up.

As the eastern horizon became lighter with the rising sun, we began to see things better. The limitlessness of how far we could see began to set in. The awesome climb we had ahead, the hugeness of what we had already done, were doing, began to dawn on us as the day did the same. I stopped and looked back to see the spectacle of the strawberry sky and thought to myself "Dave, since that is my name, this is the most stunning view of the world you have ever seen." "Yes, said I, it is." The magnificence of where we were, what we doing, the challenges behind and ahead, all combined to impress upon me that this was a pivotal moment in my then young life.

The guides called a halt for a rest break. Some men grumbled about it should have sooner, others bitched about going too slowly and taking too many breaks. The women in their modesty wanted to move away from the group to piss in private. A guy in the team ahead of mine began to puke. He complained of a head ache and feeling faint. A guide told him he was finished with the climb, he had altitude sickness. Changes in team structure were in order. Ropes were untied, positions changed, a volunteer was sought to stay with the sick man. No one on the climb was fool enough to think we could leave a man alone with altitude sickness on the mountain while we continued upward. Some one stepped forward and volunteered to stay with him. My team remained as it began, with the lazy bastard right behind me, not pulling his own weight, not helping me and bitching about how hard the climb was every step of the way.

After sorting out the problems, the guides soon had everyone underway again. We struggled on; the cross I had to bear was just behind me and not getting any easier to put up with. Some of the muted conversations in the team ahead drifted back to me. I heard some one say he did not think he could make it to the top. Others began to say they thought the top was not much farther. Of course there were complainers in the crowd, there always are and always will be. In those days, I did not yet know about the wine glass being half full, half empty, but I resolved that mine was half full, even though I did not then know the term.

Speaking of half full, my canteen was getting pretty light, as was the day, and I needed water. As the breaks became more frequent and longer, I took to filling my canteen with snow to melt inside my outer coat. I was glad the sun was coming up behind us, as that allowed me to avoid the yellow snow. I think I had already learned that old saw about "watch out where the huskies go, and don't you eat that yellow snow." Since there were no huskies in the picture, the source of the yellow snow was not dogs.

That midnight breakfast of instant oatmeal with lukewarm water had long ago been digested and burned in my struggle to move the lazy bastard up the mountain. Snacks were in order on the march. Somewhere in the snow, we stopped, the glacier struggles behind us. Crude, cold meals were broken out, sandwiches and the like, some frozen solid, others from within outer garments where they had not frozen. No one had said to put your lunch under your jacket; I just had hit upon the idea on one of our increasingly necessary breaks. As the altitude increased with each upward step, the going got tougher. A couple more people had to drop out. Someone else got the pukes from altitude sickness.

The weather for this climb was absolutely perfect. The sun was now full up above the horizon, no wind and the temperature still well below freezing. This was important as it kept the snow hard. Slush and soggy snow would make a challenging climb much harder. The snow bridges over the crevasses would not be as strong or safe.

I had no real idea how far we had come up the mountain until I looked off to the southeast toward another mountain which is over 12000 feet high and realized I could see over it. I think that was the first inclination I had of the enormity of what we were really doing. The top had to be up there somewhere, all I had to do was keep climbing and pulling the guy behind me.

Just how many people started the climb I am not sure but we lost several on the way, some so close they could probably have made it, had they persevered. Comments from the teams ahead drifted down the snow to me and my team. I kept hearing things like "we're almost there, isn't that the top yet?" and the like. But the answer was always no, it's a little farther yet. So we kept climbing and resting, climbing and resting, till we were doing more resting than climbing.

The scenery was beyond description. To the north and east were mountains unknown to me by name. In the far distance was the Rocky mountain range, cutting jaggedly into the sky. To the south lay the Cascade Range, with Mt. St. Helens, Mt. Adams and, down in Oregon, Mt. Hood.

As we looked over to the west, we could see the Olympic Mountain range and beyond it, the Pacific Ocean. In those days, Mt. St. Helens was still a mountain, not just a hill with no top. Climbing it would come a couple years later, but before it exploded. (18 May 80).

All of these other mountains looked deceptively small from my perch up somewhere above the 13000 foot level on Mt. Rainier, which is 14, 410 feet high. Looking down on the country around us, most of the near ground quite high, gave me new strength and energy for the task at hand. I wanted to get to the top and see how the world looked from up there.

This was now the third real day of the climbing experience. Our first day was spent up around 8000 to 9000 feet up on Rainier training with the equipment and guides. We needed to be able to repel up and down cliff sides. We needed to learn the art of walking with crampons, the spikes on your boots for walking on ice and snow. We needed to learn how to arrest our fall with ice axes if we started to slide down the mountain out of control. There is a whole laundry list of things to learn about mountaineering if you are going to make it to the top. And, of course, the guides are taking a look at you to see who will fail and who will make it and who will lead.

Our second day was spent getting up the mountain to base camp, called Camp Muir, which is about at the 10000 foot level. It is a small building set on a ridge with a plateau on which we would assemble for the climb. The planned assembly time had us on the plateau at 0000 (midnight) to get roped up and underway. Thus began our third day of the climb. I think few of the novice climbers in the group had gotten any sleep the evening before and that was certainly true for me. As a result, we all were operating under a level of exhaustion from the previous two days of exertion compounded by a night of little or no sleep. So hearing the whiners complain did make sense even if it was irritating.

Earlier that summer, my parents and I had made a cross country trip from Seattle to New York and back on a United Airlines DC – 8 jet airliner That flight was my first long distance air travel experience, and it was still quite fresh in my mind as we made the final assault on the mountain. I reflected upon the view from the mountain and the view I remembered from the jet as we flew across the USA. When we had departed Seattle and again when we returned, Mt. Rainier had been visible below the plane. Now here I was standing on it looking up into the blue at jets flying high overhead. The time it took for a jet leaving Seattle airport to get higher than we were was minutes as opposed to three days. So I took another step and then another.

A man up ahead called back "we are here" and we all looked up to see him with arms raised in triumph. The top had been reached!!! Now all I had to do was get to where he was. I pulled the lazy bastard hard those last couple hundred feet to get there. He was so worn down I don't think he even cared. Maybe I dragged him instead of him walking it, I don't really remember. I was so excited to reach the highest point on earth to which I had ever aspired or climbed. All I wanted to do was make it to the top.

I made it!!!! I was on top of the highest peak in the northwest!!! To this day one of the toughest physical experiences of my life and I had made good at it. The word rest does not begin to express what I needed at that point in my life. I, along with all the climbers who had made it, was beaten. All I could think to do was sit down against a rock and reflect upon the awesome beauty around and below me. One astounding sight was that of a little bird on the snow. Why was he here at this altitude? A climber near me broke off a bit of his bread and gave it to the bird, thus answering my unasked question. High over head in the azure blue sky a jet airplane flew by and I got to thinking again about that trip to New York and back earlier that summer.

We as a group had sweated swore and strained ourselves to the outer limit of endurance to get here and some of us had given up. Some were legitimately sick, some were just pansies anyway, and of course some people are just quitters for no good reason at all. But three days of intense effort had been expended to get there. The view from the top of Mt. Rainier is without compare if you are lucky enough to be there in good weather. I am very lucky. Then, as I watched that jet fly by, it dawned on me. The view out that jet cockpit window was as good as from where I was, no even better, since they were even higher than we were. And the best part of all was that it had not taken three days of grueling effort to get there.

So at that moment, in that place and time, is where and when I made my career decision. I did not have a clue how I would go about it, but I would become an Airline Pilot. And that is what I did.

Chapter Two

I was 14 years old, about to start my sophomore year of high school, with my career decision made. Now I had to figure out how to make that career happen. I sought the guidance of a lot of people, some good choices and some not so well made. This was at a time when three things were in vogue; sex, drugs and rock and roll. I soon found out that all three were a lot of fun. I became involved with my first real girl friend and got lead down the primrose path by some less than perfect examples of American youth.

My girlfriend of those days and I spent a lot of time rolling around together in the weeds, in the hay, in bed, wherever we thought we would not get caught by our parents. The school year went by fairly fast with, of course, another birthday and another hunting season, with no big deals coming along, or so I thought. It turned out that my propensities for bragging about my sexual undertakings were not just reaching the ears of my social friends, but also my parents. It developed that they did not approve of what they understood me to be doing. Of course I was blithely unaware of their misgivings and felt I knew far more than they did about what was going on in my life.

There was an incident in that school year though, which gave me pause to rethink the wisdom of the drug culture. Of course the free love, anything is alright, do your own thing philosophy, was fun, but one of the girls in my class took it too far. She did a lot of drugs, especially LSD. One afternoon at the bus, I said goodbye to her, see you tomorrow, never dreaming it was her last day alive. I knew, as did all of her circle of friends, that she was doing LSD that day, as she did nearly every day. Well it turned out that she went home, stuck a handgun in her mouth and fired. She had carried around a bullet for days and told us all she was going to kill herself, but none of us took her seriously.

The following morning at school was a day I do not recall as fun. My circle of friends all knew her very well, as did I, and now she had shot herself. I recalled that she had been stoned the previous day and resolved that I wanted nothing further to do with something that would contribute to deciding to shoot myself.

My parent's zeal for ending the relationship between my girlfriend and me was quite profound. They conjured up a plan for the summer between my sophomore and junior years in high school which was to have an equally heavy influence in my life as had the previous summer's climb of Mt. Rainier.

The plan was to separate us by force of distance. They did not like the two of us being together, so they sent me off on what turned out to be the next big life changing experience of my life up to that point. I was sent to Europe by myself for over two months. I think the idea was that if

I did not see her for a while, I would lose interest and forget the relationship. In hind sight, I think that was a rather naïve hope.

This was at a time when sex, drugs and rock and roll were not just enjoyed by me, but by every other young person then roaming around Europe. I had been sent from the frying pan into the fire, so to speak. Amsterdam, Holland, which is where I landed, in those days was wide open about drugs, sex and everything else of interest to a teenage boy on his own in a strange country. It did not take me long to link up with some characters whose names I probably did not even know then and certainly don't remember now. I was right in heaven as far as doing the very things I had been sent to Europe to avoid and separate me from. I had a girl lined up immediately after arriving in Europe and so began another fantastic voyage of discovery.

One of the first discoveries was that I could not effectively communicate with the locals because of my linguistic limitations. I could not read or speak Dutch or any other language other than English and here I was alone in Europe. This did not inconvenience me a great deal as far as finding beer or girls, but it was a challenge when asking for directions or ordering from a menu written in the local language. Today, this is not so difficult, as a lot of European countries now write things out in English for the tourists. That was not the case back then.

Another challenge I dealt with was the money. Each country had different money then, so I had to figure out the exchanges of each nation as I wandered my youthful willful way around Europe. Since I could not speak or read the local languages, dealing with these details for a kid of 15 was very eye opening.

The general plan I had at the time was to hitchhike around and go where I wished at the speed of my choosing, with a master plan of going around the entire non-communist European mainland. I got underway after a couple of very foggy days and nights of fun and games in Holland. You see I needed to get back to Holland to fly back to America by a certain date in August to return to my junior year of high school.

My next first country of discovery was then called West Germany. The Germans were a little less tolerant than the Dutch. The German girls looked every bit as good then as they do now and they certainly seemed to like me. I had a lot of fun with them, and they with me.

West Germany, as it was then known, had made a good recovery by then from the devastation of World War 2. Finding visible damage from the war was hard to do, but if I looked, I found it here and there. I met and spoke with a number of interesting people of the day. One of the more fascinating to me was an old veteran of WW 1, who had served in a U-boat. At that time, WW 2 vets were everywhere, but meeting and talking with a WW1 vet, especially a U-boat vet, was quite interesting. That meeting led me to develop an interest in other peoples and the things of other cultures I knew nothing about.

I then entered Denmark, another first for me. Entering new places became a pattern I was destined to repeat for a life time of wandering. The Danish girls looked great and were just as much fun as the Dutch and German girls. It was a great time to be young, free and on my own. Of course I had another language, another form of money, another culture to try to decipher. These challenges were becoming fun and I was finding that new nations, new people, new cultures and new places, were something I really liked.

There is a place in Copenhagen, Denmark called Tivoli Gardens, which is essentially a huge playground for adults. Some of the street people I met at the time spoke of a musician coming to play at Tivoli Gardens named Elton John. At the time he was an upward bound rock and roll musician beginning to really make his mark in the industry. I had heard of this Elton John, but did not know his music well. The street people I was in with assured me it would be a good show, so I made it to the show, and what a show it was. Elton John had a stage presence and a style of play that really captured my interest and hooked me for life into rock and roll. There were no constraints on behavior or anything else, no drinking age, no drug laws, etc. Everyone at that show had a very, very good time.

After Copenhagen, I headed on back down into West Germany, and through to Austria. Salzburg, Austria is a very beautiful city with a lovely castle on the hill above town. I found the castle to be fascinating, especially the ancient arms from wars of a thousand years ago. This was my first real opportunity to see, and be inside of, a castle. It was great and it had a spectacular view of the city and the river below. One of the fun things there was a wooden rail inside the salt mines to sit on and ride down. It was a great experience.

Upon leaving Salzburg, I made a decision to go to what was then called Yugoslavia. This was a communist country. I, as an American, was not particularly welcome in a communist nation. I think it had something to do the USA being at war in Vietnam with the communist North Vietnamese. Whatever the problem they had with me, I surmounted and was allowed into Yugoslavia. I wound up at a place called Lake Bled, which is very scenic and pretty. Now in those days, there was a book out called Europe on 5 Dollars a Day. That book is no longer in print. It was from that book that I was finding my way around the cheap drinking holes and restaurants of Europe. It also was the source of a learning experience for me while in Lake Bled, Yugoslavia.

From my book I found a word that was recommended to order in a restaurant in the Lake Bled area. I did not know what the word meant, but understood it was a local specialty. So when I saw the word on the menu, I decided to try it. Not knowing what it was, when it came it looked like scrambled eggs and tasted like meat. It was good, but what was it? I located someone who could speak the local language and English and had him ask the waiter what it was. It turned out to be fried calf's brains. Now had I known ahead of time, I would never have ordered it, but since I had found I liked it before I knew what it was, I went ahead and ate it. Another lesson learned. Don't be close minded about things you are unfamiliar with. 3 things work best when open, a parachute, a human mind and a woman's legs.

So with yet another lesson learned, I moved on down the road. Next country I got to was Italy. Now Italy is so fascinating I do not really know how to express it. Florence was fun, Venice is very nice, the leaning tower of Pisa really leans, but nothing, nothing compares to Rome. Here is the center of western culture. Here is where western civilization as we know it today began. The grandeur, the history, the architecture, it all exceeded anything else I had ever seen.

I found my way to a campground outside of town and stayed for about a week. I would go down into the city and play tourist until I could hardly walk any farther, then head back up to the camp for the night. Somewhere in there I met a young lady from Australia who was doing a summer wander through Europe like me. She was not just another one night stand, however. She turned out be able to do something no other woman ever did. She could out drink me by a wide margin. We had a great time together roaming around Rome and enjoying each other's company for about a week.

All good things must end and, of course, so did our little fling in Rome. We said goodbye to each other, promised to keep in touch and stuck out our thumbs once again. She headed for Greece and I headed up into Switzerland The road just kept calling me and I always listened, so another country became my next adventure. Hitchhiking around Europe today sounds unbelievable, but in those days, it was not the least bit unusual or surprising. A lot of young people were doing it and no one thought anything of it.

Switzerland is a very scenic country with lots of mountains, lakes, rivers and glaciers. I really fell in love with their little country. I loved the scenery and the people I met were very nice. Of course the issues of money, language difficulties and culture were there just like all the other countries I had passed through, but I was getting used to it and had figured out how to deal with these things quite well.

I wandered on up into France and hung out in Paris for a couple days, did not really like it and was soon on my way to Belgium. I made it through to Holland again. So here I was back in Amsterdam, where I had started out. I had made my way through a total of 9 countries. I had met about a million people along the way and learned a lot of things from them and from the places I had gone. I knew things about the world very few 15 year old kids ever learn. I had been in a Communist country. I had drunk enough alcohol to float a battleship and had more bed warmers than I could remember. I had succeeded in the trip of a lifetime and now needed to get back to school in USA for my junior year of High School.

Now, for the first time in my life, I got to experience the dubious joys of American customs officers at an airport.

Remember, I had passed through the borders of a lot of countries, dealt with customs officers in every one of them and had no real problems at all, including a communist country.

When I got to JFK in New York, I found out just how it feels to enter America and let me say, it has never felt good to have someone in authority believe you are guilty of something and demand you prove your innocence. A young boy alone with long hair, in need of a shower trying to clear customs did not seem out of order to me, but it certainly raised the eyebrows of the law. They were convinced I was bringing in drugs or something and I was made to feel that I was a criminal of the first order. The officers with whom I dealt treated me worse than all the other customs people in every other country I had been in. A lot of years have passed since then and I have never gotten past that feeling when returning to my country.

I have made a life time out of wandering since then and have never gotten past how unwelcome US customs agents make us feel. The number of nations I have visited and / or worked in since that first experience passed 85 a while ago, and the feeling has never left me that our own country's agents are the most miserable in the world to deal with. I am at a loss to explain this even to myself. I can only assume it has something to do with the kind of people this line of work attracts in America, or perhaps it is the training they receive. At any rate, it never has changed in all these years.

Chapter Three

My return that fall to my junior year in High School had a decisively different look for me than had the previous school years. I had now become a world traveler. I could speak intelligently about places that most teenagers had only vague knowledge of and fewer still could find on a map, yet I had been there. I knew about drinking in countries where it was no big deal, I knew more about girls than all the other boys in my class combined, and I had a goal. The idea of flying for a living was still very much alive; indeed it was stronger than ever, because I had seen the benefits of that line of work. I could, in a day's time, go half way around the world, into cultures, places and peoples the friends I had at the time could not comprehend. This goal had to be met and this was the year I would get it underway.

Along came another hunting season, which is to say another birthday, since I was born in hunting season. I got into the fields and forests numerous times that fall. This was facilitated by the fact that I now had a learners permit to drive, so I would drive on all sorts of excuses. It was never hard to find someone to hunt with. My father and I spent many a day outdoors together. Along came the magic day that I turned 16. Now I was old enough to have a license instead of a learners permit. This also meant I was now old enough to get serious about flight training.

My father and I went down to the little country airport near where we lived and talked to a guy who was a flight instructor. He talked at length with me about what to do to become an airline pilot. He talked about the work load, and the money. I did not have a clue where I would scare up the money or how, but my father assured me we would figure it out and I believed him.

That winter, when the weather permitted it, I would fly with the instructor for my lessons. I did not fly very often, which did not help me progress and I don't think my fascination with girls helped much either. However I did it, I don't know, but finely one day my instructor told me I was ready to solo. This meant I was to fly the plane by myself, with no one else aboard. For the first time in my budding aviation career, I would actually be the pilot, not the student. This was a momentous occasion in my young life. To say I was excited is an understatement. We had been through spins, stalls, steep turns, engine failures and every other thing you can do in a single engine plane, but now I had to fly it myself or die. I chose to fly.

The training after that continued and I made my share of mistakes. One thing in particular that was a near miss was going on a long cross country flight alone with no thought for fuel. When I arrived at the second airport, I happened to notice the fuel quantity indicators showed empty so I asked another guy on the ground if I should continue or get gas. It turned out I only had 3 dollars in my pocket and no other way to get gas, so I asked for 3 dollars worth of regular and was on my way. I lived through it.

I had the bright idea one day of flying low over some very interesting activity on the ground. Now this was at a time when the Vietnam War was raging. The ground I was flying over was an army base and what I was looking at was live fire war games involving tanks, infantry and artillery. For some reason, the army did not like my circling over their little games at about 500 feet. This lead to my having a very unpleasant conversation with the FAA in the Seattle office. My Flight Instructor also had a not very nice conversation with the FAA and he wound up losing his Instructor license because of it. To say our flight home from the meeting with the feds was not fun together would be another understatement.

My friends of those days did not include any student pilots or sons of pilots or anyone who gave a second thought to flying. I was alone socially in that I wanted to do something my friends could not understand and did not care about. That was alright, as I was very comfortable alone. Remember, at 15 I had traveled alone through Europe. There was a fascination among girls for flying, I think. At least there has always been among the girls I have known. So, of course, there was a girl who came along in that school year who liked me and I her. We had a good time together.

As always, the school year ended and my feet were itching to get gone somewhere. I came up with the grand plan of going hitch hiking on the Alaska Highway. Now that required I get a few things together such as a decent back pack, as the one from the last year had not survived for further service. I had worn it out in the woods hunting.

Well the back pack and a few other things fell into place and I found myself standing in the rain with my thumb out in Anchorage. I got picked up by a lot of people and invited to go do all kinds of things having little or nothing to do with hitching or flying.

One character I got picked up by told me he was a bush pilot. Now this was a term I needed to have explained and soon I had my life goal further refined. A bush pilot fly's little airplanes to remote locations in Alaska and takes hunters and fishermen to remote places to hunt and fish and acts as a guide for these outdoorsmen. I made up my mind that bush pilot thing would be my future. It took a while, but I got there.

Another strange turn my life took about then involved a group who called themselves The Lord's Land. These people had gotten their hands on a working dairy farm and brought in a bunch of losers from around the USA to pray and sing and generally run a good farm into the ground. They offered me the chance to hang out with them for as long as I wanted to do so. Well of course I took one look at the girls available and immediately came to the conclusion that farming, or something that started with F, might be fun. So I hung out there and had a good time with them for a while. One of the guys in the picture got his nose out of joint with me about one of the girls and I decided it was time to exercise my thumb some more, so I hit the road. Going north from Palmer, I found my way to Mt. McKinley National Park. To this day, that stands out in my memory as one the most beautiful places in the world. I wandered on up to Fairbanks and soon found my way down to Front Street, where all the bars and whore houses were in those days. Now I cannot say exactly what happened, but as best as I can recall, the police and I had a disagreement over something which resulted in them putting me in a cage for awhile. Although this was not my first run-in with the police, or the first time in a fight, it was my first time in a cage. I did not like being caged, as the hitch hiking in there was a little slow.

When I could do so, I wandered on down the Alaska Highway toward Canada. I got to a little town called Toke and I thought I had found the most aptly named place in the world. I got picked up by some guys in there and we spent 3 or 4 days together hanging out and having a good time. We traveled from one beer store to another, never allowing ourselves to get thirsty. We crossed the Canada border, how I don't know, but we did it. We would see a creek or river or lake along the road and stop, break out the fishing gear and the beer and that was it. We were stopped until the next day. Fish cooked over an open fire is delicious. We would catch grayling, trout or what ever we could. We saw salmon in a creek and caught one with our hands, only to find they did not taste very good after they had been in fresh water for awhile.

We parted company and I was alone on the Alaska Highway with my thumb out and nothing going my way. In those days, the Alcan Highway, as it is sometimes called, was dirt. I could hear a car or truck coming long before I could see it. So I was sitting along the road watching a mother bear and her cubs when I learned a little something about bear's hearing. I could hear nothing but the noises the bears were making when suddenly mom stood up on her back legs and twitched her ears around. She left out a woof and the cubs disappeared into the bushes. She soon followed and a good 3 or 4 minutes later, I heard the vehicle coming that she had gotten concerned about. I was impressed.

I found myself in Whitehorse, Yukon after a few days on the road by myself. Here I found a girl who thought if she let me have a shower at her house, maybe I would be alright. I

21

have no idea if she thought I was alright or not, but the next morning I was on the road again.

I hitched on down to the end of the Alcan, at Dawson Creek, in northern British Columbia, where there was pavement again. The hitching got a little easier because there were more cars and people so my pace picked up a bit. I passed on down through the length of beautiful British Columbia from north to south, back into the USA. Here I got to experience the dubious joys of US customs agents again. This was now my second time of entering the US alone and the agents who greeted me were no less unpleasant then the last bunch. I was just a long haired 16 year old kid traveling alone. They did not make me feel welcome at all.

When I got down to the Seattle area, I got picked up by a man in a Volkswagen with the right front seat laid out flat. This was at night and he seemed very, very interested in me, to a point where, when he told me how much fun I would have if I went to his place with him, I suddenly realized I would rather be walking. I let him know I wanted out of his car but he did not want to hear that and kept driving. I stated my position more clearly and he kept driving and telling me about the "good times" we would have. I had a strong sense that the good times he had in mind were not good times I wanted to share in.

We were going in the direction I wanted to go in, but I did not care, I wanted out of that Volkswagen. It was very uncomfortable holding my backpack in front of me and not being able to lean back. His insistence that I go with him to where ever it was he wanted to take me did not make my comfort increase. Now bear in mind this was at a time when young people in the greater Seattle area were going missing with a frightening frequency. Well he just would not listen to my lack of enthusiasm for his plan, so I figured I should come up with a plan of my own. I resolved to shut up and ride for a minute while he talked about the "good times" we were going to have.

My plan evolved into the kill or be killed idea. I suddenly and very loudly shouted "HEY" in the Volkswagen. He turned abruptly toward me and I hit him in the face as hard as I could, breaking his nose. He let go of the steering wheel, put both hands over his now bleeding face and moaned. I reached over, grabbed the wheel with one hand, the emergency brake with the other, and steered the car to the side of the road. I got out with my pack, reached back into the car and grabbed a handful of his hair. I pulled his head over toward me and punched him in the face a few times, as hard as I could. He was no longer interested in these" good times" he had been so enthusiastic about before.

Many years later, about 20 or so, I was reading a book called Stranger Beside Me, which is about a man named Ted Bundy. The details of him at the time, the vehicle I got picked up in, the greater Seattle area while the "Ted murders" were occurring, all lead me to the conclusion that I may well have been picked up hitch hiking by Ted Bundy. Of course I will never know for sure, and I cannot prove it either true or not true, but I believe I may well have ridden with one of the most well known serial killers in American history.

Well, I was soon back home with my parents and getting ready for the next school year. My father had come up with the idea that a moose hunt in northern Alberta would be the thing to do that fall. Now hunting is very educational, and it was his view that for hunting, it was OK to miss school. This is a view which I shared at the time, and still believe to be true. My father and I and another fellow we had hunted with previously on several occasions set off for Canada with our rifles and equipment. More wandering for me was always a good idea. We took about three days to get up to extreme northern Alberta in the truck.

The idea was for us to hunt hard every daylight moment we could, so I was shown an immense field into which moose were supposed to come every evening and early morning. This became my hunting area. Well there I sat on the very edge of the field, my back to the forest, watching for moose to come out. I heard noise in the brush behind me and turned around silently to see the source of the noise. I tried to look as far into the bush as possible, expecting to see a moose. As I moved my eyes right and left, looking far into the bush, I suddenly saw, right in front of me, a huge black face just 10 feet away from where I sat. This was a bear and he was very, very close.

I raised my rifle and held a bead on his eye. I spoke out load and said "you can turn and leave or take another step and die". He made the wrong choice for himself and I shot my first bear. I then stepped it off and found he was just 10 feet from the rock I had been sitting on. Had my first shot wounded him or missed, there would have been no second chance. Knowing how to shoot well, not just talk a line of crap, but really shoot well, was a skill that had just saved my life. I owe this to my father for having taught me a good skill. This skill, in years ahead, would again save my life several times over.

So here I was alone in the wilderness, 16 years old, with my first bear killed. I set to the task of cleaning the bear and getting him ready to go for a long ride in the truck. When finished, I walked on back to our camp and hung out till my father showed up at dark. He saw I was bloody from cleaning the bear and said "you got one?" I said 'yes, but it is not a moose". This now required us to figure out how to get me a license for a bear before the Fish and Game boys showed up. We successfully resolved the issue and we wandered on back to the USA several days later. I did not get a moose, but I did have my first bear.

When we took the skin to the taxidermist to have it turned into a bear rug, the taxidermist stated it was the best skinning job he had ever seen. All these long years later, I still have and treasure my first bear. A lot of other trophies from hunting all over the world fill our house, but that is one I value very highly. It is one of the many hunts my father and I shared over the years and I am glad we did them all. I wish there could have been more.

Back at school, I had now done yet another thing that my classmates could not really grasp .For my friends of the time, wandering just was not that important to them. They were a lot more interested in getting stoned and drunk than in growing up. I began to seek the company of more adults and not dealing with the kids of my own age. I wanted to talk about the world, about flying, about hunting, just about anything that involved expanding my horizons. I had found my circle of friends to be confining, boring and unfulfilling. I was now a confirmed wanderer and I had left most of them behind, emotionally speaking. There was, of course, a young lady who I really liked for that school year. We did a lot of things together and I think we could have gone a long way into the future, had an unfortunate incident not occurred. She hounded me to ride my horse, not just an old plug, but my personal horse. His name was Sonny and he was a very high spirited, powerful, fast, strong willed horse and he only allowed me to ride him. I had the strength and skills to deal with this very spirited hot blood, but few other people could do so. I stupidly allowed her to get on him. I could tell immediately it was not a smart choice, but chose to not speak up. Sonny took off at a dead gallop with the girl just barely hanging on, totally unable to do anything at all to control him. He soon threw her off. She hit the ground hard, breaking her arm. I had made a stupid decision I should not have made and she was hurt as a result.

I took her home to her father, who was a state trooper. He was not at all happy with me and that pretty well ended our relationship. I saw her many years later and we both agreed we wished things had turned out differently. She had no hard feelings toward me.

Somewhere in there I turned 17 and it was determined that I needed to find a job and start acting like a young adult instead of a foot loose and foolish kid. There was a roofing company near us I could walk to and from for a job, and soon was busting my ass as a hot roofer. Now this is a very dirty, physically demanding, dangerous job. My starting salary was a tremendous $1.65 an hour for the physically toughest job I have ever had. I soon became a lot stronger and tougher, to the point of which I got to where I could take 2 90 pound rolls of tarpaper, one on each shoulder, and climb up a ladder with them both.

Of course the inevitable day came when I got hurt. The pipe which brought up the bubbling hot liquid tar slipped and I got burned with hot tar. No words I can express do justice to how much fun this wasn't. I soon found myself in the hospital, getting the now hardened tar removed from the cracks in my skin which had formed from the burns. This was not the most pleasant experience I have ever had. I lost several days of work because of my burns and thus the income. Not that $1.65 an hour is a lot of money, but that was what I earned. When I returned to the roof, the guys all said they were amazed I had not run right off the roof in pain and shock. Apparently, that is fairly common with severe tar burns. The good news was that I got a raise, up to $2.00 an hour.

It took a lot of hours of sweat and labor to earn enough to rent the plane to work on my license to fly and my goal sort of languished for a while, until I could figure out another plan.

The summer I was 17 and working as a roofer, I learned another very important lesson regarding other people. Two of my buddies at the time and I came up with the bright idea of going off to Montana for a few days of fishing. Now we really did not have a clue as to where we would really go, we just thought it would be nice to go wandering, so we did. The truck we went in was a older clunker and of course it gave us problems.

We were up on the very top of the continental divide when the engine decided to throw a rod. That means it was done running until some major maintenance got done. Three 17 year old boys with no tools to speak of and very little knowledge, was not a great team of experts. I took off hitchhiking into the nearest town to find a junk yard to get parts for the engine.

On the way down the mountain, I got picked up by another young guy, perhaps 20 or so years old. He listened to my tale of woe and gave me some suggestions on what to do. His advice turned out to be good and he dropped me at the junk yard. I found the parts I needed and headed back out towards the truck, way up in the mountains and many miles away. Along comes the same car as the young man had been driving, this time with two guys in it. Now the driver was the father, a man about 45 or 50 years old. When I opened the door to get in, the father said "I don't usually pick up hippies, but my son says you are OK".

The two of them took me to my truck and towed us back to their house, using the family car and a chain they had in the trunk. We three were told we could stay in the family house, use any tools we needed out of the garage, and have meals with the family.

Three days later, we had the truck fixed and were ready to go. As a gesture of gratitude for the family's generosity, we offered to work for them for a few days to repay the favor, as we had no money. The father said "no, you guys just go on down the road and return my favor to someone else in need." I have never forgotten those words and the deep meaning behind them. To this day, I have tried to remember to follow that man's example and return his favor to those in need.

Chapter Four

High school graduation was now behind me and I was working still at the roofing company. The pay had improved a little by this time and I had gotten my first car. It was a real good car. It had been crashed and needed a lot of work to get it working and looking decent. I bought it for the outstanding sum of $150.

Now my taste for hard physical work had not improved and I needed to hit the road again. A very large and angry fellow had let the word out that I was in need of being killed by him. Now I felt that his threat was real and I did not wish to find out if I was right or not. As had become usual for me by then, it involved a girl. The large, angry fellow was figuring to marry the girl in question and she had been stupid enough to tell him about an affair between her and me, hence he thought the thing to do was to kill me.

One of my friends from the roofing company and I hatched a plan to keep me alive that involved going to Mexico for a while to lie low. On the road again, this time in my $150 car instead of hitch hiking. My friend and I set off with a case or two of beer and a vague idea to stay away from the greater Seattle area for quite a while. We thought the thing to do was to winter out down in Mexico and let the large angry fellow cool off.

Once out of Washington State, we slowed down a bit and took our time to go anywhere we chose. We had left on a rainy Friday night with virtually no planning or thought to anything other than just getting me out of the area quickly. We wandered around Oregon, stopping to fish and get beer and sleep and get beer. We finally got to the California border after 4 or 5 days and stopped some more and got more beer and fooled around as much as possible. It took us two full weeks to get down to Los Angeles, a trip we could have made in two days.

Calvin had a friend in the Navy down around LA somewhere. We found his apartment and just sort of moved in on him and his wife. We stuck around for several very inebriated days and nights, until the guy's wife told us to get the hell out now. We listened to her advice and left.

It took us 4 days to get to the Mexico border, down south of San Diego. This is a drive which could be done in 2 or 3 hours. We wandered around in Tijuana for a couple of very different days. Neither one of us could speak any Spanish, but it was not too hard to figure out what the hookers and pimps were saying. We quickly learned the Spanish word for beer and a few other key activities available to us for a small fee.

Somewhere in Tijuana, we wound up in a conversation with a group of Mexican police and got the distinct feeling it would be best to head back into the USA real soon. I don't pretend to understand the minds of police personnel, but they took a real dim view of our having firearms with us in Mexico with no permits. Rather than lose our guns, we split back to California. Come to think of it, I believe we might have lost more than our guns, had we not run back into USA.

Now we needed to have another plan, because we would not go anywhere without our firearms and we could not go into Mexico with them. We got some beer and hit the road in my $150 car, heading east along the border toward Arizona. We agreed that wintering in Tucson might work for us about as well as Mexico since we were sure we had not been followed from Washington. That large angry fellow was still on my mind and I had no real desire to see him anywhere.

It took us several days and several cases of beer to get to Tucson We hooked up with some shady characters as soon as we got in town and agreed the thing to do was to get jobs. Since we both knew how to roof, that is what we did. My friend lost interest after a couple days and stuck out his thumb. He had no reason to stay away from Seattle, so he left to go back home. I was sleeping in my car and living very marginally in the parking lot of the roofing company. One of the guys suggested I try to get a room in the dorm at the university with some other people to spread expenses.

I holed up for a while with one of the roofers in a tiny little one room shack of a house. That did not last too long and I went to the university to look for housing. That panned out for a few weeks, but of course, along comes the next girl. I was in a bar one night and met a nice looking woman who invited me to come to her house after the bar closed for another drink. Of course I said yes and followed her home.

The next morning, early, she shook me awake and very urgently told me to "get up, get up, my husband is going to be home any minute." I did not need to be told twice. I went from sound asleep in her bed to behind the wheel of my car in seconds flat. I got about two blocks away and passed a pickup going the other way. I watched in the rear view mirror and he pulled into the driveway I had just left. I went to look at my watch and found it was not on my wrist. I had left it in her bedroom and did not go back to get it.

I lost my job as a roofer and now did not have a pot to piss in, a window to throw it out of or dirt for it to land on. I really like to be able to shower once in a while and needed to find a place to hang out. I wound up living with two chicks in a tiny trailer for a while.

I was down and out financially with nowhere to go and no way to pay for anything. When the girls wanted me to pony up for the rent, I did not have it. They invited me to hit the road and so there I was again.

I believe this is about where I hit my personal bottom up to that point. I was up a grapefruit tree, stealing fruit and got caught. The tree was in the yard of a church and the Pastor had caught me. I felt like the stupidest fool in the world, to be stealing food from a church. He and I had a long discussion, which lead me to the next major move in my life.

I went down to a part of Tucson where all the military services had recruiting offices and had several conversations with the recruiters. The various offers of the day all had plusses and minuses, and I chose to go with the Air Force. So, on a whim, feeling low down, I joined up and was given a class date to report for basic training. The recruiter could hardly believe his luck because when he asked if I was willing to go to Vietnam, I just said "yeah, sure", which was not something most recruits were saying to that question. Now I had a real future plan. I was going to go to Vietnam and become a hero and gain my pilot's license on the government. That dovetailed nicely with my penchant for wandering.

That day, after leaving the recruiter's office, I met a girl who said she was from Washington and wanted to get back to that state. She took me home for the night and we made a plan to head back up to the Northwest in the next few days. She was willing to pony up some money which I did not have and she had some other assets I liked pretty well also. Our general plan was to hit the road in my $150 car pretty soon and go over to California and north up the west coast where she wanted to go.

Exactly how long we partied around, I no longer know, but we eventually got underway. We took about 3 days just to get to southern CA, as we were always stopping to take a break from driving and do things that we found more fun. We eventually got to Washington State and went to her house, where I met her mother. I did not get the feeling her mother really wanted me around by the next morning. Some comments that I overheard lead me to believe the best thing to do was to go wandering on down the road, this time without the girl.

I wound up back at my parents house, broke and depressed. I never heard another word about the large angry fellow who wanted to kill me, so apparently my plan had worked. I was right back the next day working for the roofing company, just filling time until my class date for the Air Force. Somewhere in there, I managed to hurt myself, so my feet hurt terribly when I had to stand up for long periods of time. This was a problem that was not going to just go away and it had far reaching, long term effects I could not have foreseen.

Chapter Five

It was the almost time for me to go to the service and I was running around with some good drinking buddies. We partied as hard as possible, drinking everything that had alcohol in it and chasing anything that looked female and human. This practice lead to another one of those little problems with the police.

It was the night before I was to report to the Air Force. We had gone to the store to get more beer, but it was after 2:00AM, which is when the stores were required by law to stop selling booze. The store guy just said "sorry, it is after two, I can't sell it to you." Well, of course we were already well on the way to drunk, so we just walked out with the beer, the hell with paying if he was going to be that way. The store guy followed us out and got the license number of my $150 car, called the police, and waited to see what would happen next.

The cops went to my parent's house at about three in the morning and asked for Dave. My father said I wasn't there, but he had a good idea where to look for us. He was right. The police entered the house we were partying in without knocking and accosted us for a variety of things, not the least of which was stealing the beer. I do not think they liked the looks of my buddies or me either.

One thing lead to another, and we soon were going for a ride in a cop car. The genius's had the bright idea to take us to the store and have us identified. The store guy had not seen the driver, so of course that is who went with me. I could not get out of it, as I was the one in the crowd with the brilliantly blonde hair. Just before getting in the cop car, I suddenly had the brain storm to put on glasses lying there in the house. When we got to the store, of course the store guy did not recognize us. He had not seen the other guy with me at all because he had been the driver, and I had not been wearing glasses in the store. The brilliant cops had no choice but let us go when the store guy said he did not recognize us.

After the nonsense with the cops was over, I went home and told my dad I was ready to go the service. He was a little angry, to put it lightly, with me for the BS with the cops. He did not take kindly to being bothered with their crap at three in the morning. Can't say as I blame him.

He took me to the enlistment center, where we all took the oath to "defend the country, the flag and the girls" or something like that. There was a memorable moment in that room when we all had to drop our pants for an asshole check. This involved two guys going along and looking into everybody's ass for whatever they thought they would find.

Well along towards the back of the room, they told a guy to "bend over and spread em".

The next thing I heard was a guy saying "God damn, look at all that shit." This was followed by a deep, obviously black voice saying" what did ya'll expect to find, ice cream?" Of course the place just fell apart.

So began my wandering on down to Texas for basic training with the Air Force. I was put in charge of the contingent of guys going on the plane by some genius and immediately got things going in the right direction with a stop by the bar in the airport. Once on board the plane, I let the flight attendant know I thought she was the best looking woman I had ever seen, and told her my little group and I were going to Texas to work for a while off shore where we would not be able to get a drink for quite a while. She took pity on us and gave us all the booze we wanted. My little group of guys thought I was the coolest guy around.

When we got to San Antonio, no one met the plane. As leader, it was my decision to go to the bar. After all, where more logical to wait for someone than the bar? That is where we were sitting with drinks in front of us when the MPs showed up to arrest us, especially the leader. (That would be me.) This was not a real good way to start a career in the service.

When we got to the base, I was given some special love and attention by the Sergeant to whom I was released. In view of his size and rank and my insecurity, I chose not to fight him. In retrospect, I feel that was the right choice. I just don't like those damn cages.

As always, I worked things out with the people controlling my life at the moment, and was soon in with my unit in training. Here comes that damn foot problem again. The most exciting thing to do in basic training is stand in one place, not moving, while some jerk yells something at you that you could care less about. The jerk doing the yelling holds your future in his hands and he has about a seventh

or eighth grade education. Not a real appealing picture or
future from my perspective.

After a few days of this standing around on my horribly
painful feet, I had enjoyed about all the enjoyment I could
enjoy. The sergeant noticed my limping and brought me in
for a one on one conversation. I could barely walk, let alone
run or do any of the other fun things he had to make us
do.

Now I am going to find out about military medicine.
This should be fun. The hospital at Lack land Air Force
base is huge and I could not really get around too well. I
eventually found a foot guy and he did not care if I lived or
died, so he told me I had some grim choices to make. Now
remember, I wanted to be there, this was not just another
party for me. I could either have an operation which could
easily cripple me for life, or accept a medical discharge.
Just like that, my draft status went from 1-A to 4-F. This
means I had been the top choice for being drafted to go to
Vietnam, now I was physically unfit for military duty. I am
sure there are a few Vietnamese who are alive today because
of that choice.

I spent the next few weeks in the hospital, awaiting a
discharge I did not want. I had lots of time to think. I was
not permitted to read anything except the Uniform Code
of Military Justice, or religious material. I chose to read the
Bible, the Koran, and the Torah from cover to cover .In the
Bible, I found a verse that says something like "have a little
wine every day for your belly's sake", whereas neither the
Torah, nor the Koran, mentioned this at all, so I decided
being a Christian was the thing to do. After all, I cared
about my belly.

While lying there in the hospital bed with lots of time
to think, I thought about some of the really bright people
I had known up to now. It occurred to me that none of the

truly intelligent people I knew were like these dumb shits in the Air Force telling me how to make a bed and how to polish my boots. The difference was education. I resolved to use this new found revelation and get one.

Yes, I had a high school diploma, but that clearly wasn't going to be enough, not if I wanted to rise above being a roofer or an enlisted puke in the military. That next logical progression was to go to a university or something and graduate. There is a community college in Washington State which has an aviation program. The gig is to get a two year degree in commercial aviation, which is what I did. What I failed to do was understand the difference between an AS degree and an AA degree. This misunderstanding would wind up costing me a lot of money and at least a year of my life. I cannot say today whether I failed to understand what was said to me, whether I was lied to, or whether I just made an honest mistake, but the result was a lot of pain in the ass for me.

Chapter Six

After my discharge from the USAF, I chose to take the money, not the ticket home and, surprise, stick out my thumb. From San Antonio, I headed west, thinking about some of the girls I had known in Tucson. Some of the rides I got were a little interesting, but basically, I got blasted all the way across Texas, New Mexico, and into Tucson, AZ. I had a pocket full of money and no constraints upon me, so I thought the thing to do was to get as blasted as possible while chasing down all the girls in Arizona.

Of course there was a guy who did not like me messing with his girl and I got an itchy set of feet about the same time. Funny how that coincidence keeps coming up in my life. So it was back to wandering again for me. I was deeply depressed about the turn of events with the military. I truly wanted to go to Vietnam and shoot little yellow guys. That was my plan and now it had gotten taken away from me.

I wandered on up to Washington on my thumb, having a lot of good times along the way, but never seeming to shake that depression. I sank to lows I had never really known before. No one night stand could do it for me. The girls along the road just seemed to flow together and so did the drinking. However, there was a night in Utah which stood out.

The girl and I had met at the Mormon Church, and she thought the thing to do was for me to go back to the ranch with her and spend the night. When we got back to the ranch, she wanted to head out into the orchard for privacy. After we did the dirty deed, I happened to inquire as to her age. When she said she was fourteen, I decided there was a better place to spend the night than under the same roof as her father. This decision motivated me to find my way back to the high way and continue my wandering.

The next morning, I got picked up by a guy who asked if I had a driver's license before he would give me a ride. I said yes and got in. It turned out he had bought a car in Salt Lake and needed a second driver to get both cars back to Spokane, Washington. Well, that suited me just fine, so off we went. He did not even know my name, just trusted me that I had a license. It happened to be true, but he never asked to see it.

What he had bought was a 1955 Chevrolet, a very powerful car, which even back then, was classic. He gave me the key, and I gave the car the throttle. I buried the speedometer, which indicated up to 120 MPH, so of course I have no idea how fast I got it up to. After several miles of high speed, I let it off to about 80, and, after several minutes, the owner showed up in the rearview mirror. He did not like being left behind.

I drove his car to Spokane, shook his hand, and hit the road again. I hitched on over to the Seattle area, went back to my parents home, and immediately started planning my next wandering. I was back at the roofing company, depressed and unfulfilled. Wandering just filled the hole like nothing else could. Of course we were drinking and partying just like the old days, but now the fellow roofers had a different slant for me. They were nice guys and we had a lot of fun, but I needed more. I just did not want to be a roofer all my life.

You guessed it, I hit the road again. This time would be a marathon. I had started out hitching in Texas, up to Washington. I resolved that I would go to the extreme ends of America this time. I headed back to Alaska.

On the way up to Alaska, I had a few adventures, nothing of any real significance. I found, on the way up the inside passage, that this place called Alaska, really held something for me. I resolved that my life would be lived out in this magnificent, wild place. I did not like the stupid Canadian laws about no handguns in their country, which was an issue while transiting to Alaska, but, like everything else in life, there are ways around that.

There was a night somewhere along the road that stands out. I got plastered with some other guys and got a little more than I bargained for. I got horribly sick for three days. This was just not fun. We had eaten some food that was not right and I paid the price with my personal misery.

I found my way back to that spectacular place, McKinley Park, and saw again why I was alive. Seeing the most beautiful place on earth could do it for anyone interested in the real world. Yes, I know, this was not Hollywood, and for those who live their lives in that world, you will never understand anyway. For those who understand, no explanation is necessary. For those who do not, no understanding is possible.

I went up to Barrow, which is the most northerly town in the world, something like 400 miles inside the Arctic Circle. Here I met for the first time, the Eskimo people. They seemed to have a good view of life from up there on top of the world, just hunting, fishing, and living off the land. This also marked the first time I ever saw the ocean frozen over. Many times I had seen fresh water frozen and had done my share of outdoor ice-skating, but up until then, I had never seen a frozen ocean.

After returning to Fairbanks from Barrow, I shuffled on down the Alcan, passing through Yukon, a most wonderful part of our great big, wonderful neighbor to the north, into beautiful British Columbia, just like before. Lots of drunken, crazy days followed lots of drunken, crazy nights of wandering. I was still deeply depressed about having not made it in the Air Force.

Now the dubious privilege of dealing with US customs came up again. They never seemed to accept the fact that I was a habitual wanderer and just let me go through. They still don't.

Back in good old USA again, I wandered on back by mom and dad's place again, then headed east. My goal now was to get to the eastern most extreme of America. I stuck out my thumb and headed out of town.

Most people who pick up hitch hikers ask the same basic questions: where have you been, where are you going, and how long have you been on the road? I had learned by then to not give any real answers to this shit, because it was not their business. My life was my life, and if they wanted to get to know me, they needed to buy some booze. If they happened to be female, another way was to get their feet in the air.

I got picked up by a woman in North Dakota. She really did not have a clue about geography, so I convinced her that the best way around the great lakes was through Canada, to the north. The next morning, we woke up in a wheat field with some farmer with a shotgun in his truck telling us to get off his land. We did what he suggested.

We wandered on up into Manitoba, to Winnipeg. There we found a place to procure some supplies. That would be a liquor store. The next few days sort of flew by in a blur. Somewhere in those days, I was driving and ran over a skunk. Now for those of you who have never had this experience, you are lucky. A skunk has the ability to emit the worst chemical odor of any natural animal on earth. When I hit this critter, he did not go gracefully. He sprayed his scent all over the bottom of the car as he was dying. We traveled together for the next several days in odoriferous misery.

I do not know if she ever believed that I did not mean to hit the skunk, but I am sure she never forgot those days with that smell. We wandered on into New York State, by that big waterfall, Niagara. She dropped me off someplace after a really great night of, well, you know. I did know her name at the time, but I do not remember now, and I doubt she knows mine. Suffice it to say I appreciated all the times she and I shared, both good and bad.

I showed up at my grandfather's farm and got on as a farm hand. It was summer time and he needed a hand. I worked through the hay harvest, the toughest time of year for a dairyman. I met some girls at the time and had a good time. You know who you are and I thank you for the good times. I hope you feel the same.

It did not take long before those old feet of mine got to itching again, so I said I will see you later to those I was leaving, and hit the road again. I hitched on up to Maine, to Acadia National Park, on the coast of Maine. In that park, I met a couple who wanted me to go with them for a drink and whatever. We soon wound up in the sack as a threesome, the first time I had ever done this. It was a little strange, having the boyfriend watch while I did his girlfriend right after he had done her. She seemed to have a good time and that is what mattered to her. Actually, I had a good time too.

Now it was time to turn around and head west, back to the best part of America. I was born in Oregon, raised all over the west, and I have never lived east of the Rockies. I don't want to and don't intend to.

This heading west from Maine as a hitch hiker may seem a bit daunting, but I was looking forward to the road. After all, I am a committed wanderer. So out went the thumb, into the rain, as I closed in on the last leg of my marathon trip across USA.

I got a ride down into Massachusetts from Maine, and then was stuck under a freeway bridge for the night. Eventually, I got a ride from someone down into New York City. Now this is a place I really don't care for. As I was walking down the road, some street blacks got around me and started trying to talk me into going with them to God knows where. Not surprisingly, this did not interest me at all. I managed to shake off all but one, who kept telling me about the things he wanted to do to my asshole. No was an answer he did not want to hear. We came to a street vendor selling hotdogs and sausages. This street scum wanted me to buy him one so he could suck on it. I saw that as an opportunity. I told the seller to sell him the dog of his choice, here is five bucks, keep the change, and ran for my life.

I now wanted to get out of NYC as fast as possible and did not care how. I asked a cop for directions to the bus station. He turned around and pointed at a huge skyscraper and said "it's right there." I got on the next bus to New Jersey, it being to the west, and kept going.

I eventually got back to Washington State after a few more good times. Nothing really stands out, but the road is always good for me. There was a time in Wyoming when I got picked up by some guys in a van who knew how to travel. Within five minutes of them saying get in, I was drinking their whiskey, and sharing their good times. We wandered for a while. Somewhere in there, they dumped me out along the road, so drunk and fouled up I did not know I was back on the road.

The next morning, I awoke in a ditch by the side of the road with a roaring hangover. When I tried to sit up, I found out with the top of my head, that I was under a barbed wire fence. Having one's head cut open first thing in the morning with a hangover is not my first choice of ways to start the day.

After getting situated, I looked off down the road and could see a neon sign, so I headed for it. The sign turned out to be a breakfast place, so I walked in and asked the greeter "where am I?" She seemed a little put off at my question, but informed me I was in Montana. Now the last thing I remembered was that I had been picked up in Wyoming, so here was a real life case of not even knowing what state I was in. I went into the men's room and found my head to be bloody, which may have been part of the problem for the girl at the door. So now I had learned what state I was in health wise and geographically. This is always good info to have.

The road kept calling and I had a date to be back in Washington State for, so I kept moving west, on back to Mom and Dad's place. No real adventures came along the rest of the way back home, a point I reached just three days before I was to start college.

Now when I got to Mom and Dad's place, my father accosted me about some girl I had never heard of and I told him as much. He was very angry with me and demanded to know how I could get some girl pregnant and not even know her name. Since I truly did not know what he was talking about, he relaxed a little and told me of a phone call he had received from an angry father regarding his pregnant 14 year old daughter and my having been named by her as the guy who did the deed. This was not good. I asked if the guy had left a number to call back. The answer was yes and I did so immediately. Her father ranted and screamed about how he was going to take everything my family had for having knocked up his daughter. When I explained that I was a legal adult and did not have a pot to piss in, a window to throw it out of, or dirt for it to land on, he calmed down and forgot the whole thing. I do not know whatever became of the girl and her pregnancy. I assume the pregnancy ended at some point, they usually do.

Chapter Seven

The enrollment process was no big deal and I was soon ensconced in the dormitory. Right off the bat, I found out this was a co-ed dorm, which meant there were girls and boys in it. This sounded like something I could get to like.

The curriculum was built around the flight training program, mixed with academic courses like meteorology and math and science stuff. The idea was to get an Associate of Arts degree in Commercial Aviation. This is where I screwed up and misunderstood about the AS versus the AA degree, as mentioned before. I started taking classes for the aviation side of the house only and blew the other classes off.

Private pilot ground school was intended to get the student prepared for the Private Pilot written exam, and , of course, to teach him something about basic flying knowledge. The instructors were all men, some of which I liked better than others. I was to come to know all of them well. Out of our class of budding aviators, there were two women and about 40 men. Not to get ahead of myself, but both of the women, 100% of the women in my class, were dead in aircraft accidents within one year after graduation.

Of course I met and liked a few girls in those days. One that comes to mind was an employee at the student cafeteria. She and I did a few things together, until her mother told her to drop me. No big deal, by now I had figured out that the best red snapper still swims in the sea, and if you want to catch fish, you must keep your worm in the water.

One night I was out acting stupid and getting drunk when I had yet another run in with the law. An Officer pulled me over and asked me to get out of the car and do the roadside drunk test. My answer was honest but not too smart. I told him "shit officer I can't even do those things sober." Probably not the most well thought through words to use, but that is what I said. The Officer in question asked where I was trying to go and I pointed to the dormitory and said "right there." He let me drive to the dorm and park my car with a stern warning not come back out that night. I followed his advice.

The flight training went along well and I was able to pass the Private Pilot written test, a major milestone. The other guys in the class moved along at about the same speed as me, with one outstanding exception. There was a guy who was doing a tremendous amount of dope all the time. He kept failing tests we all had to take, while we just kept on moving forward. I, like the others in my class, suggested to him that if he did a little less dope and a lot more studying, maybe he could catch up. This was an idea he never seemed to grasp. At the end of the first year, when the rest of us all had our first Pilot licenses, he had nothing passed at all.

So now it is the summer between freshman and sophomore years of college and I have a Private Pilot license, Single Engine Land. This means I can fly little single engine airplanes in good weather, but could not legally accept money for doing so. Also, the land part of the license restricted me to wheel planes only. No float planes yet, so I resolved to get the float rating that summer. Up in Seattle, on Lake Washington, is a business called Kenmore Air Harbor. This is a float plane base and in those days, a student pilot could show up and take training to get his float rating.

I showed up with a couple dollars in my hand and said I wanted to get rated in floats. The office girl told me what to do and who to talk to and soon I was on my way. Now writing from many years and many ratings later, I still say that getting my float rating was the most fun rating I ever got. The things I had to learn about float flying served me well in other types of flying as well. One huge difference from wheel planes is that you have no brakes. You have to think out in front of the plane or you will crash into a dock or the shore line. Another big difference is the wind. Just like with a boat, no brakes and nothing to keep you from drifting sideways with the wind. Where this really becomes tricky is in a river with current and wind in different directions. Once you shut the engine off and drift, you have to have already made the right decisions or you are screwed, blued and tattooed.

So with a little training, I was soon beaching and docking and drifting just fine and the instructor turned me loose with the plane, to go practice my skills solo. Well now this is where it really came home to me that girls like pilots and planes, because I went to another lake and landed and went to the beach in a crowded public park. I soon had bikini clad girls all over the plane and they were asking questions that I was only too happy to answer, usually with the word "yes."

In between the training days in floats, I was still slaving away for the roofing company, busting my ass for about $4.00 an hour. This had become more than full time. I was often on a roof for 14 to 16 hours a day, so the over time helped. I don't mean to imply that I liked it; I just mean I was beginning to make a little money. The same group of guys still worked there, some of them around 50 years old, and I just could not see myself doing that hard labor for the rest of my life. These were good men, hard working guys who had no education and no alternative but to keep busting there asses as long as their bodies held out. Every day I worked with them, I thanked God for giving me the vision to see the future I did not want and the means to escape it.

My second year of college got underway in September of that year and so did hunting season. I was out of the dorm now and living in a house. Now, for the first time in my life, I started actually living with a girl. She was a beauty and we had a good time together for quite a while. She taught me many things I did not know and needed to know if I was ever going to have a real relationship. I know it sounds hard to believe, but I was trying to grow up in the way I dealt with women. At this point in my life, bed warmers were a dime a dozen, but meaningful relationships just kept slip sliding away. With this new development of living with a girl, I was plowing new ground. One regret I have from those days is not being straight up and honest with her about my life up to that point. It would have gone a lot better if I had not BS'ed her so much about my past.

Be that as it may, that second year of college I tried hard and made the Dean's list of honor. This was not because I was a great student, but rather because I wanted to fly for a living. This was my only chance since things had not worked out with the Air Force. When I got the notice I had made the Dean's list, I made sure it got sent to my parents. They thought it was cool and I took them flying in little airplanes several times.

Around Moses Lake, Washington, in those days, was great hunting for birds. My school schedule allowed me to go out in the morning before class, hunt a limit of birds, go to class, then go back out and hunt another limit of birds. Fish and Game never caught me and my girl friend routinely joined me, so we ate a lot of birds in those days. There reached a point where we could not put any more birds in the freezer because of our hunting success. Canada goose is very good.

There was an instructor on the staff named Mr. Downing. Mr. Downing had been a pilot since the 1930s and had served in the Army Air Corps during WW2 as a B-17 pilot. He had done his 25 missions over Germany and knew how to fly. He had given me my Private check ride and now, in my second year, gave me my Commercial check ride. After it was over, (I passed), he said "you are going to go on and be a commercial pilot someday. Why don't you learn how to make landings, since that is the only thing passengers care about?" I thought about his suggestion and moved on to the next phase of training, which was my instrument rating.

About this point in the game, along came the first death of a colleague, a thing in aviation which I had not reckoned on. One of our instructors, in my mind one of the best, was out with a female student, a first year one. For reasons known only to God and them, they crashed in a field, the plane burned with them in it, and the flight program was out an instructor, a plane, and a lot of confidence. Up to that point, no one had been killed in the program.

My personal reaction was profound sadness. Of course I could not know then how many friends and colleagues I would lose over the years in aviation, so this first one was a real shock. To add insult to injury, the girl in question was good looking.

Well things moved on and we continued to fly toward our licenses and graduation. The day came for my instrument rating check ride. Mr. Downing administered the ride, just the like the two before, Private and Commercial. At one point on the approach, he took the radio and told the tower to have a 747 do a 360 for spacing because this was a check ride and he did not need them on our tail. The tower complied. Lesson learned for me. If you don't like the way things look, request something different.

We got through the check ride alright and he gave me the speech about landings again, but I passed. So now I had a Commercial Pilots License with an instrument rating in single engine airplanes with a float rating. I was definitely moving up in the world of aviation. The next step was the Multi-engine rating, which would allow me to fly airplanes with more than one engine.

The Multi-engine course was about 10 hours of flight time in a light twin. There were several things about twins I needed to know, such as what happens if an engine quits on the runway while the other is still working on takeoff. Or what if one quits in flight while the other is running? These questions kept me thinking throughout the Multi-engine training.

Somehow I did it and graduated with my Commercial Pilots Licenses, Single and Multi-engine Land, Single engine Sea and Instrument ratings, with an AS degree in Commercial Aviation. Now had I been smart, I would have done an AA degree, but I was too busy chasing girls and my dream, to pay attention, so I got an AS instead of an AA.

In order to build time as a pilot in the civilian world, you have to put in your time as a Flight Instructor when you are starting out. Yes, I know there are exceptions to this, such as the guy who had a father as the vice-president of Alaska Airlines or something, but for the average Joe, this is how you do it. So I got my Flight Instructor license and set out to teach beginning students how to fly. I gained my 300th hour as a pilot on my Flight Instructor check ride. At the end of this, I was issued a license to teach other people how to fly airplanes. This was something I barely knew how to do myself, let alone teach to others.

I soon had a job at a small flight school and got my first students. I believe it safe to say that in my first 100 hours of teaching others to fly, I learned more than they did. In the door walked a woman about 20 years older than me. She looked pretty good to me and she wanted to learn how to fly. I got the student and we soon were deep in conversation about what she needed to know, what she needed to do, to buy, etc, before she could obtain that Private pilot license. Not that I had a clue, but I was her instructor.

She seemed to like me and responded well to my instructions. She was a public school teacher, a profession that never has paid enough to its practitioners. We hit it off well and the day came when she reached for my crotch and performed a great blowjob on me in flight. Now this was a first and I enjoyed the hell out of it. Shortly thereafter, we joined the mile high club .Quite a number of firsts were being fulfilled by me at that point in my life. I had no way of knowing it then, but this mile high club membership would turn out to be something I would find myself re-establishing numerous times in the future.

The student in question went on to become the first student I trained from the initial walk in the door through her Private Pilot license. We continued to see each other for several years after her license was in her hands. She became heavily involved with the 99s, a women's pilot organization.

As I said earlier, that first 100 hours as an instructor were very informative for me. There was the guy who panicked in the cockpit on me at very low altitude when I simulated an engine failure on takeoff. This was one of those times you would rather read about than experience. The gentleman in question was a carpet layer by trade, so he was very strong. When I shut down the engine, (single engine plane) he freaked out and yanked the yoke back into his lap as hard as he could with both hands and held it. He would not release it on my command, so I had to hit him, hard, to get him to listen. The alternative was to have the airplane stall out and fall onto the runway. This would commonly be known of as a crash. This occurred at about 100 feet off the ground in a takeoff. I was a little pissed. Somewhere along the road, it has come to my attention that people trying to kill me really piss me off.

Then there was the guy who lied to me about his experience level. Being young and naïve, I believed his line of crap and let him fly farther into the approach than I should have. This was in a tail wheel biplane with an open cockpit. This fellow did not know his ass from a hole in the ground about flying tail wheel planes and he had lied to me, which now made us into a hole in the ground. By the time I said "I've got the airplane", it was too late and we ran off the runway, out of control. I poured the power to the engine, just got off the ground and hit the trees. Now a propeller does a fair job of cutting trees into firewood, but the thing is, that is not its intended purpose. We soon hit the ground again, this time with the prop in the dirt, the tail in the air, and the gasoline pouring out of the now broken upper wing directly onto the smoking hot engine. I thought my ticket was punched right then and there.

Now, for the first time in my life, I heard sirens coming for myself and it is not a great thing to hear. The ambulance drivers could not see the plane down in the bushes, drove right by and kept going. There go the fire trucks, following the ambulance. My lying student was now lying on the ground in total panic, muttering nonsense to himself about being killed. I am not sure if he meant by the crash, by me, or by his own stupidity for lying to me. At any rate, I went up onto the runway and a fire truck came along. The driver wanted to know if I had been in an airplane crash. I replied in the affirmative and indicated where the student was.

That night, many hours later, the girl friend I had at the time put her head on my chest and exclaimed in alarm at my heart rate. I felt my own pulse and found the rate of beat was extremely high. This was after about a 4 hour discussion with the FAA concerning the pros and cons of flying tail draggers. The FAA people informed me that, as the instructor, it was my responsibility to verify the student's qualifications prior to allowing them to land the plane. The fed suggested that I get some more training in flying tail wheel aircraft before I resumed teaching in them. That seemed like good advice. So now my first airplane crash was behind me.

The flying school I was working for changed management a while after the crash and the new guy did not need me around anymore so I moved off to my second job in aviation, another flying school. Here I was not just an instructor, but started doing charter flying as well. This would entail flying passengers to other places and moving freight around as well. In the summer time it would involve spotting for forest fires. This could prove to be quite interesting, as it often involved getting right into the smoke column and being tossed all over in the rising air currents at low altitude in among the mountains with poor visibility. Sometimes the excitement would be added to by the observer getting air sick and puking in the plane while I was trying to fly in the smoky environment.

After a couple of good years there, I needed to move on, although I did enjoy it. I wound up at another flight school, teaching flying and doing charter flying. It was at this school that I gained enough flight time to get my Airline Transport Pilot license, Single Engine. I turned 23 and got the rating at about the same time, that being the minimum age at which you could get that license.

With yet another rating to my name and a significant amount of flight time, I could expect my resume to be taken seriously, so I sent it off to a few flying outfits in Alaska. Remember, I had had the dream of being an Alaskan bush pilot all these years. Now the time had come when I was going to make good on my efforts. The call I had waited years for came soon and I was on my way.

Chapter Eight

In the Arctic in April, it is still quite cold. Lower 48 residents would call it winter. To those who live there, I don't mean weekend tourists, I mean those who live there, winter is over but to most people outside Alaska, below zero at night is still winter. It was into this climate that I now arrived to take up what turned out to be the most enjoyable, not the most money, but the most enjoyable, years of my life as a pilot.

The residents of the village of Kotzebue, Alaska are almost all Eskimos. A few years before, I had been a weekend tourist in Barrow, but had not then gotten to know any Eskimos. Now I was living with them and it did not take me long to find them a fascinating people. These people had been living in the harshest environment on earth for about 30000 years before Europeans came along and started telling them how to live. One thing I quickly figured out was that these guys did not need outsiders like me to tell them how to live. On the other hand, they had a lot to teach me, if I was willing to listen.

This business of being a bush pilot had a few hazards involved. One thing that struck me was the ever present question in single engine planes of what to do if the engine quits in flight. Now out over the wilderness of arctic Alaska, an engine failure would very likely mean your death, if not in the crash, then from the brutal cold afterward. Assuming you got out of the crash and into the cold without serious injury, there were the hungry carnivores around. Yes, this means wolves and griz. The uninformed will be saying something like griz are asleep all winter, but those who know will remember that griz often get up in mid winter and wander around in a bad mood and hungry. Wolves, of course, are hungry all the time and stay awake all the time.

My very first morning in Kotzebue, my new boss wanted to get to know me, as I had been hired over the phone, sight unseen. Now it developed that he owned a bar named the Arctic Inn. It was into this smoky, dark, smelly hole in a snow bank that we went for the get acquainted discussion. The owner, my new boss I had just met, smelled of beer and gave all the indications of a man already under the influence, this at about 9:00AM. I had a somewhat different view of how my first day of being a bush pilot would go.

The owner told the ugly old woman behind the counter to give me a beer and told me to order breakfast, so I did. We had breakfast together, washed down with several beers and a lot of BS about flying. Along about noon, he said something about going out to see how well I could fly. Now I assumed he meant the next day, as I was definitely under the influence and he was well on the way to drunk. Wrong answer, he meant we were going flying now, so finish your beer.

Off we went to the office I would be flying out of for the next several years. I was beginning to get some definite images of this flying gig that did not fit with my preconceived notions. One hard and fast rule that apparently did not apply here was the old law about 8 hours from bottle to throttle. My previous employment as an instructor had always required a neck tie. This was another item from the lower 48 I would not need in the Arctic, so I traded my tie for a gun and moved on.

We got into an airplane, taxied out and did several instrument approaches to the airport, as well as several landings. We headed out over the frozen ocean to find a place to land out in the country so I could demonstrate my skills on the tundra.

It all turned out well and I was welcomed aboard as the newest pilot with a huge amount to learn about flying single engine planes in the Arctic.

This was at a time when navigational aids were just beginning to show up in the bush, so a great deal of finding your way around involved memory and looking out the window at very low altitude in bad weather. Structural icing could be a factor any day of the year.

The learning curve for a new guy was nearly vertical. I came to a conclusion fairly quickly about this bush flying game; a pilot here had to make choices every day. You had 3 of them: You could get out, you could get killed, or you could get good. I am sitting here years later writing this book, so you can draw your own conclusions.

On the social side of things, life with the Eskimos was unlike anything I had ever experienced I cannot say how it is now, this was years ago, but suffice it to say that the female Eskimo is the most morally open minded woman on earth.

They used an expression "oly-pop" meaning beer. It was a common thing for them to come in the bar and say to me "you buy me oly-pop, I be your wife tonight." So for the price of a couple cans of beer, you would have a wife for as long as you wanted to keep buying beer. If you went to work and there was no beer in your house, she would be gone when you came home. This, of course, was no problem; you just went to the bar and soon had another wife or two.

A short time after I got to Kotzebue, I was sitting on a bar stool by a woman who had a huge black and blue bruise on her upper arm. I asked how that happened, how had she gotten hurt. She replied that her boyfriend had given her an Eskimo abortion. I did not know what that meant, so she explained to me that she had told him she was pregnant, so he had swung a shovel at her stomach as hard as he could to kill the baby. She had instinctively moved her arm to protect herself and the handle had hit across her arm. She then hoisted up her shirt to show me a horrible bruise, all purple, blue and black, with a triangular cut in the middle of her stomach. The cut was from the corner of the blade. The bruise covered most of her stomach. She related the details of this successful abortion as though she were telling me it was snowing outside. Essentially no emotion, just the way it was in her world.

This was my introduction to the callous domestic violence which was then and probably still is a large part of the daily lives of these people. When sober, the Eskimos are wonderful, loving people. When they are drunk, senseless, vicious domestic violence becomes the norm. Over the years I lived with them, I saw so much of it, I became cold to it and ceased to care about all but the most graphic. There was no point in me, an outsider, trying to tell people of a different culture and race, how they should live their lives according to my standard. That would only serve to alienate me from them.

Not too long after starting to fly the bush, I was summoned out into the hanger by the chief pilot for a conversation. As a new hire, I was sure I had done something wrong and was being fired for some reason. The chief pilot sounded very serious as he explained to me that he knew I was a new comer to the Eskimo way of life, but he was sure I would figure it out soon. One detail of life as a bush pilot he thought he needed to explain was that it was my responsibility while living with them to help breed them out of existence. This was a responsibility I accepted with enthusiasm.

August of my first year in the Arctic came along. That means fall to an Alaskan. It also means hunting season. The outfit I was flying for was owned by a Master Guide certificate holder. I was soon recruited to be an assistant guide. I took hunters out and showed them where to find big game animals such as caribou and moose and griz. My float rating paid off now because we had a float plane which was used almost exclusively for taking out hunters and bringing them back in. I had reached the end of my personal rainbow. I had fulfilled my dream of being a bush pilot and guide.

Guiding was done mostly in August and September, while the flying went on year around. We flew every day and every night in all kinds of weather and for all kinds of reasons. Sometimes it would be gold seekers into mine sites, sometimes it would be freight. We always had the local bush people riding around with us in our planes. The girls would always want to join the mile high club, so I helped quite a few attain membership. One day, I departed a tiny little village out on the extreme end of the Seward Peninsula with a young woman who wanted to become a member of the mile high club. I agreed to help her do this, so we set about the act. Well I cannot say exactly how things unraveled the way they did, but when she was finished joining the club and started getting her pants back on, I noticed mountains out the window. Now I was familiar enough with that part of western Alaska to know that the mountains did not look like that anywhere on the Seward Peninsula. I could not place where we were, but it was not mountains I had ever seen before. It took a while of thinking and guessing, but the bottom line is that we had flown across the Bering Straits and were in the Soviet Union.

I took the decision to leave the area without any delay. I took up a heading back to the east toward Kotzebue and got down to about 50 feet above the pressure ridges in the ice so the bad guys might not see me on radar. We made the trip back across the Bering Straits into more familiar country as fast as I could make that little airplane fly. Nothing came of it and the young woman in question had her mile high club membership.

The guiding was the most exciting thing to do because most of the clients were quite wealthy, egotistical, self-centered blowhards who were quite convinced that they had odor free feces. Of course it required a fair degree of self-control on my part not to inform some these characters that their shit did in fact stink. We had one character that showed up in pressed slacks, dress shoes and a dress shirt and tie. His idea of outdoor, cold weather gear was a light wind breaker jacket Remember this is an arctic hunt out on the tundra with no buildings of any kind for a week or more. When we laughingly questioned him about his gear, he arrogantly stated it was the guide's problem, not his.

Another example of the kind of garbage some of these individuals would come up with was the guy who spent most of the night before going out telling me and anyone else who would listen, just how great a shooter he was. His line of BS was so extravagant, even I, as a new kid on the block, realized no one could be as great as this fellow was in his own mind. His line of crap ran to the point where he had himself believing he could outshoot US Army snipers, why he was even better than an Olympic shooting team member, in fact he could probably outshoot any human being on earth, or some such nonsense.

There did not seem to be any limit to what this shooter could do. He probably even thought he could shoot around corners. Too bad I didn't ask him that, I might have met a magic man. Well the other guys had this blowhard's number before I did and I got to take him out for a moose. As best as I can figure it, the only thing he was skilled at shooting was his mouth. He certainly was head of the class for that skill.

We went out and found a decent bull moose, nothing to go in the record books, but nothing to be ashamed of either. We agreed to put the stalk on this moose, and I soon had the world's greatest shooter in a nearly perfect shooting situation on an unsuspecting moose. The range was smack on 100 yards, little wind in our face, level ground with a rest for his worlds finest custom made $50000 rifle. As near a perfect shooting situation as a hunter could ask for.

When I gave him the go ahead to take the shot, he immediately started farting around with his body position, his rifle, the rest he had, grumbling to himself about God knows what, and generally wasting time while the moose feeds placidly in front of us. This is not going to last. Wild animals rarely stand still for long and this moose was not going to stick around if he heard, saw or smelled us. I whispered to him go ahead and take the shot, which an idea he had not come up with. Now this is the world's finest shooter, so it would seem like he should know when the shooting situation was right. It was perfect. Somewhere around 15 minutes elapsed between the world's finest shooter getting into position and finally taking the shot. You guessed it, he missed.

The moose is not going to hang around, you would think, but all this guy did was pick his head up, take a few steps, flop his ears around trying to figure out what that loud noise was, and go back to eating. The world's greatest shooter was at a loss to explain this phenomenon. I did not need an explanation; I needed him to get in another shot before the moose headed for Canada or someplace else far away. My hunter took this opportunity to express a stream of verbal filth which compared favorably to a drunken sailor on a weekend pass. Maybe he thought he could kill the moose with BS.

After several minutes of diddling around with his rifle and making profane excuses for the miss, he finally fired a second shot, and missed again. The moose reacted about the same as before, looking around, flopping those big ears around and trying to figure out the source of the noise.

Just as before, the world's greatest shooter expressed a stream of profanity the likes of which I had not heard since basic training in the military, and blamed his custom made rifle. He had paid more for that rifle than houses were going for back then. I think it was operator error.

After extensive nonsense and wasted time, he got off a third shot, this time connecting with the moose right where the hair met the hoof on the rear foot, breaking the animals ankle. The wounded moose had now figured out what all the noise was about and he did not like the experience.

The moose now did indeed start to head for somewhere far away, in an effort to get away from what had hurt him. I knew my hunter's shooting skills did not match his BS skills, so I raised old Roy Weatherby's finest product (that would be my rifle), and killed the moose. This was no big deal for me. I am not the world's greatest shooter (there can only be one), but I do know how to shoot. The alternative to me killing it would have been for a wounded animal to escape onto the tundra to wander for days in agony before being pulled down by wolves or a griz. As an ethical hunter, I could not allow that to occur.

We walked over to moose, checked out the antlers and agreed it was a good one. My genius hunter chose that moment to inform me he was not tagging it, as he had not killed it. As his guide and pilot, I informed him that would be fine, when you walk into town from here, if you live to get there, good luck with the Fish and Game boys. Wanton waste of big game will get you 10 years free room and board, courtesy of the state of Alaska, in a cage. I cannot explain it, but the idea of walking across 100 miles of tundra alone without a clue as to which direction to head in seemed to affect this hunter's judgment, and he changed his mind about that tag. It has never ceased to amaze me how stupid some otherwise intelligent people can be.

When we got to town, in my plane, he tried telling the owner about how he was not going to pay for the moose, since I had in fact killed it. This resulted in a call to Fish and Game. One of their officers showed up and gave our hunter a little advice. The long and short of it was the hunter and his moose got on the Alaska jet down to Anchorage, we got paid and I had another lesson learned.

There reached a point in there somewhere when it dawned on me that life in the Arctic was very confining, given the isolation, which was part of the game. The Eskimo people do not value education very highly, as it does them no good on the tundra. This was different from how I felt, so I resolved to get more education for myself. Now remember, I had gotten an AS degree in commercial aviation at a Community College and did not yet know this degree was essentially worthless. I asked the owner if he and I could have a talk out in the hanger. He agreed and we went out in the hanger. This is where we went to speak somewhat privately with the owner or the chief pilot or somebody if we did not want an audience. I asked the owner if we could agree on my going out to the lower 48 to go to college again, with the understanding that I wanted to come back when I could. He seemed to think I had done a good job up to that point, so he agreed to the plan.

Thus I left the Arctic, which I had come to love, and wandered on down to Washington to try and finish my education. My intent was to enroll at Central Washington University as a junior, thus having two years to go. I believed my AS degree would suffice for the freshman and sophomore years. Learning that the university was only going to count about 4 classes from my Community College days was one of the biggest let downs I had experienced up to that point in life. It ranked right up there with not being able to make it in the Air Force. The school's view was that I was welcome to enroll, but it would be as a freshman with only a handful of useable credits to my name. A much cheaper alternative (I was paying my own way, it was how we did things back then), was to enroll at another Community College and complete an AA degree, so that is what I did. This wound up costing me thousands of dollars and another year of my life spent in classrooms I had not planned on. In those days, to just get an interview with a major airline, a 4 year degree was mandatory. The degree could be in basket weaving or clay modeling, it just had to say BS or BA on it.

Chapter Nine

I got settled into a rental house in Yakima, WA and started down the road of completing my AA degree at Yakima Valley Community College. I soon had a white girl friend with a job and things were looking alright. Being a college kid again and living in a real town with roads and cars was hard to readjust to. No one I dealt with had any real understanding of life in the Arctic. The average day time student was a couple years younger and a lifetime less mature. None of them had ever done any wandering and only one student I met on campus, a guy, could hold much of a conversation about anything of interest. I, on the other hand, was the subject of intense interest because I had already lived a life beyond the scope of most people's imagination.

Just being a pilot was fairly cool, but having been a bush pilot in the arctic and having lived with Eskimos was apparently fascinating to both students and faculty. The classroom discussions seemed to always wind around back to what I had been doing up north. I found it rather easy to BS my way through the classes and get passing grades. For the first time, I was taking college level classes that had nothing to do with flying. These were basic second year courses I needed to pass if I were to ever get that all important BS degree I needed to go on and fly with a real airline.

Money got real tight at one point in there and I had to make a trade I hated to do. I owned a rifle which I cherished and the owner of the house wanted his rent money. Having no other available alternatives, I traded that rifle away for a month's rent. Doing that got me through to the end of the school year.

Somewhere in there I got together with my old friends from my roofing days and saw right away that I could never go back to those days. They were still nice hard working sincere guys, but my life had passed them by and that was very plain for me to see, if not for them as well. We really had nothing in common any more except the past and the conversations of those memories soon got thin.

The school year ended in June for me and it was time to head back up north to the country and the job I loved. I did not have that coveted BS or BA degree, but I did now have an AA, which the university would accept as having completed the first two years of my 4 year degree. I made a call to the owner of the company and he told me he wanted me back yesterday, when can you get here, so I got my things together, bought a ticket on Alaska Airlines, and headed back.

After check in at the counter, I was sitting around waiting before going through security when a man walked up to me and said "you want to buy a rifle?" Of course I was interested, so I said "what kind of rifle?" His answer, "a 12 gauge," told me he did not know his ass from a hole in the ground about guns, as a 12 gauge is a shotgun, not a rifle. I smelled the chance to get a deal, so I said "let's see it". He told me to wait right there, he'd be back. In a few minutes, he showed up carrying a gun case. I opened it up and saw a beautiful, brand new, Belgian-made shotgun. I knew it was worth quite a bit of money and asked him how much he wanted for it. When he said "fifty bucks", I knew I was dealing with a fool, so I told him I only had forty. He gave me a line of crap about needing fifty, so I told him to go sell it to someone else. Of course he backed down, I gave him forty bucks, and he disappeared into the crowd. I walked back over to the counter, showed the agent my ticket and said I had forgotten to check this gun. He gave me a box to put it in and a ticket to claim it with when I got to Kotzebue. So I acquired a valuable shotgun for forty bucks that was worth far, far more than that and went back to the great land of Alaska.

Chapter Ten

Upon getting back to the Arctic, I went right back to the life I had come to love, flying, fishing and females or something like that. The Eskimos were very glad to have me back in their midst and I was glad to be back with them. The flying was exciting and the life was very comfortable for me.

There were a lot of domestic violence experiences and most of them have all fallen into the background with time, but two events stand out from those days which I just have never shaken.

One involved a young man and a 12 year old girl. He was 18 and demanded she have sex with him. She refused his advances. He had gotten his hands on enough booze to get so blasted he did not know what he was doing, and that is the common thread through all of these experiences.

As bush pilots, one of us was required to remain sober every day and night of the year for medical evacuation emergencies. On this particular case, I had the duty and got called out. A state trooper met me at the plane and away we went. You see, there is no law enforcement in the bush, so the law had to come out from town. In an area with no roads, planes are the only link with the outside world.

When the trooper and I arrived, the girl was presumed dead by the local villagers. She had been very badly beaten by the boy, breaking numerous bones in her arms, ribs and face. She had been badly cut several places with some sharp object, such as a knife or axe or perhaps a broken bottle. As if that were not enough, he had then poured gas over her and set her on fire. The trooper checked her over and was surprised to find she was still alive. He immediately sent me back to town to get a doctor, while he stayed there to do his job.

I told the doctor on the way back out to the village about the girl. When we got there, he went right to work trying to save her. The trooper asked me if I was willing to take the boy back to town alone and turn him over to another cop when I got there. I said "yes, but I cannot guarantee the prisoners safety." The trooper looked at me for a few seconds, nodded and said "I understand, I will finish up and then we can go back together."

I took the doctor and the girl back into town and returned for the prisoner and the trooper. When I got to the village, the prisoner and the trooper were waiting for me. I overheard the boy ask the trooper how long he would be in jail this time. His answer was that it would be a very long time.

Several months later, I had the same doctor in my plane for another emergency and I asked him about that girl. He answered me by saying that he had served as an army medic in Vietnam and had never seen a human body in that terrible a shape that was still alive. She had been saved.

I saw an awful lot of needless, callous violence in those days, all of it involving alcohol, but that one event still stands out. Another event came along about this time which was just as disgusting. I got called out for another emergency in another village. This one involved a dead baby. When I flew over the village to alert them I was there, the parents heard the plane and started out to the strip. When I parked the plane and got out, they were walking out with the dead baby. They were carrying it by one ankle, its other leg flopping and its hands dragging in the snow. The little body was naked and blue.

I asked the drunken father what had happened to the baby and he claimed he did not know. When I took the little body from him, I could clearly see the bruising all over the body, and the back of the skull was crushed in. Obviously, its head had been smacked against a wall and neither parent seemed to care at all. When I asked them for something to put it in, the father went off and came back with an empty beer box. I guess that was a fitting coffin for the little guy.

I took the body back to town and gave it to a nurse at the hospital. Nothing ever came of this obvious murder of a baby. Such was life with the Eskimos.

At various times in the arctic, we would be sitting around in the office with nothing to do but BS, and on one of those occasions, the discussion revolved around where we thought we would be killed in our line of work. It was a foregone conclusion none of us would live to be old pilots. The chief pilot went to the big map tacked to the wall and stuck his finger on a spot, telling me that was where he thought I would be killed.

Several weeks later, I got called out for another med evac in the middle of the night and went up to the village of Shungnak with a nurse. When we got there, it was for an old lady that no one knew the age of, but they thought she was in her 90s somewhere. After I got her loaded in the plane and threw the engine cover over her to keep her warm, I asked if she was OK. She said yes and away we went.

After about 30 minutes or so of flying, right over the spot where it was predicted I would be killed, I heard her let out a groan. I thought nothing of it until we got to town. An ambulance met my plane when I landed. I pulled the engine cover off of her and asked how she had enjoyed the ride. The medic stuck his fingers against her neck, turned to me and said "she didn't hear you, she is dead."

As we all know, there are three things that must happen in life, the first being conception, then birth, and finally death. Well as a bush pilot, the conception part happened frequently in my plane. One trip I flew down to Buckland, I had a young girl in the front seat with me, about 11 or 12. She turned around and looked over the seat into the rear of the plane several times, giggling each time. I got curios about what was so funny back there and looked back to see her older brother and sister screwing right behind me.

On another med evac flight one dark and cold night, I went after a gunshot victim. He was shot through the guts and was bleeding pretty badly. I got the locals to give me some toilet paper and patched up the holes as best as I could. While this was going on, some guys brought in a teenage girl in labor. She was about 15 or 16 and they said it was her first. She was screaming out in fear and pain and begging for help.

There was no way I could put two stretchers in my plane, so I walked on back to the plane and got on the radio. (This was before the days of cell phones.) When I finally got somebody to hear me, I requested another plane to come out and help me with these two med evacs.

When I heard another plane over the village, I was surprised to see my chief pilot was the pilot. When we got to the school where the victims were, he took one look at the situation, said "I've got the gun shot, see you later," and took off, leaving me with the girl.

I rounded up 4 sober guys to help me, rolled the girl onto a stretcher and we carried her down to the plane. She had quit screaming for a few minutes, so I figured this was the time to go. As I was opening the door to the plane, one of the guys holding the stretcher slipped on the ice, lost his balance and fell down. This in turn caused the other guys to lose control of the stretcher and the whole works fell on the ice, stretcher, girl and guys, one big pile of laughing guys and a screaming girl. I told them "the hell with her screaming, get her in the plane, I will go anyway." So we got her loaded on the stretcher and into the plane and off I went.

As you have guessed by now, she went into labor again in my plane and when we got to town, I had two passengers instead of one. That was probably the most screaming I have ever heard during that flight.

Thus I have had the three requirements, conception, birth and death all occur in my plane, during flight while working as a bush pilot.

I also watched a friend die in the water one fall day. In single engine wheel planes, one cardinal rule is to never, never be more than power off gliding distance from shore over water. Float planes are a different issue, but in wheel planes, this was one rule wise pilots never violated. The idea is that if you lose your engine, you will be able to glide to a landing on land rather than ditching in the water.

The ice had not yet formed in early September, but most of the guys in the area had already taken their planes off floats and converted them back to wheels for the winter. My friend was coming back to town and had to cross a body of water about a mile wide, so of course he should have been at least 1000 feet or higher over the middle. He wasn't and, sure enough, at the worst point right over the middle, his engine quit. He called the flight service and stated he was going to crash on Pike Spit. I was close by and heard his call, so I headed over to watch the crash. His next call was that he wasn't going to make it to Pike Spit; he was going into the water. The weather was good, so there was no real reason to be so low.

I could see his plane before he hit the water and I watched him go in. As I circled over the plane, I saw the heads in the water of the occupants as they climbed on to the tail of the plane. The front of the plane sank because of the engine, and then the rest of it slid beneath the waves. Now there were just five heads in the water.

As I continued to circle over head, I was talking to flight service and advising them of what I was seeing. They managed to scare up two float planes and get them in the air. The number of heads in that freezing water had dropped to four, then three, as I continued to circle over head and direct the float planes into where the swimmers were. I knew the pilot well, had relieved him of about $50 the night before in a poker game, and now I was watching him die.

The number of visible heads had dropped to two and then I could not see any at all. The first float plane to arrive was just below me over the water and I told the pilot I had not seen any heads for several circles now, but this is where they were. Just as we were passing over each other, I happened to see a head in the water. I told the float pilot "there is one right below you." He spotted it, chopped the power and landed in the waves by the swimmer. He managed to fish the woman out onto the float and dragged her aboard. Like all Eskimos, she was carrying her baby under her coat on her back.

They took off and landed right in front of the hospital at the beach. The woman and her baby were the only survivors from the flight. A long time later, I think about six months or so, the FAA came to Kotzebue and awarded me a hero award for saving these lives. As I explained into the TV camera at the time, I had done nothing that any other bush pilot in the same situation would not have done. I think if it could be done over, I would do nothing any different. All I can say for sure is that I wish the dead pilot were still with us and I had never had to be a hero. His body was never recovered.

Chapter Eleven

One of the hunts I was a part of consisted of four guys, all of them bow and arrow enthusiasts. They came into town ready to head right out into the bush. They did not even care about going to the liquor store first. I was impressed. Most of the hunters we worked with were not this well prepared.

All four of these guys had everything together and their equipment was well organized. They only carried one firearm, a 12 gauge shotgun, for camp protection from griz. Otherwise they were strictly bow and arrow hunters. The plan was for them to spend two weeks on the tundra for caribou, then one night in town to reprovision, then two more weeks on the tundra for moose.

We took them out to where they were to hunt and wished them luck, leaving them on their own until we came back. As well planned and prepared as they were, we knew they would be fine and did not make a plan to check on them during the hunt.

We came back when the two weeks were up and they were ready to go, their equipment packed and stacked, with four record book quality caribou heads. These were good hunters.

We took them and their animals back to town, they were ready to go on time the next morning, and they were not hung over. All they really wanted to do in town was get some supplies and a shower.

We put them out in prime moose country and left them again for two weeks. When we came back for them at the end of the two weeks, the equipment was packed and stacked and they had four record book quality moose heads. All this with no rifles, only a camp protection shotgun. I was impressed, these were good hunters.

At the other extreme were the guys we put out for moose on a river. I pointedly told them to get the camp off the sand bar, up onto the tundra and away from the rivers edge. Of course they were smarter than I will ever be and camped right on the river's edge, exactly where they should not be. Griz love to cruise up and down the edge of the river, looking for things to eat such as dead fish or caribou that have drowned in a crossing or whatever.

Had these genius's listened to a few words from me, no problems would have come along, but, like I said, these guys were far smarter than their guide would ever be. They killed a nice moose and brought the trophy right into camp with them. During the night, while they were sleeping in the tent, along comes Mr. Griz. He found that wonderful free meal lying right there exactly where it should not have been, and helped himself to it.

The next morning, our brilliant hunters went berserk with fear and frustration about the missing moose and the griz tracks where it had been the night before. Being of sound minds and good judgment, they did what any self respecting genius would do, they pulled out a couple bottles of medicine and drank themselves into stupidity. They formed a plan to sit up and wait through the night for the griz to come back. This plan was helped along with several bottles of Arctic antifreeze, more commonly known as whiskey.

One thing wise hunters never do is mix whiskey with firearms, but this bunch was much smarter than most, so they proceeded to get plastered, with loaded guns, and wait for the griz. Of course the griz could smell what they were doing all the way down wind for a couple miles, so he just waited till they all fell into a drunken daze and passed out.

When they came to the next morning, there were fresh griz tracks all over the place and they had never heard or seen a thing all night. Now they were genuinely scared and they had pretty well used up all the medicine the night before.

Add to this mix the fact that it was raining and/or snowing and sleeting all the time and these guys were not real seasoned outdoorsmen. I forget whether it was the third or fourth night, but Mr. Griz visited again and this time he took all the remaining food and dragged the only camp stove they had brought with them off into the bush where they could not find it. Since there are no trees out on the tundra, that means there is no firewood either. Now, for the remainder of the hunt, some of the world's smartest hunters had no heat source and no food. They forgot all about hunting after this and just sat in their tent waiting for the plane to come back and rescue them. The only moose they had gotten was gone and that was the only game they saw.

When I arrived to get them, they almost ran into the still spinning prop as they charged to the plane. They were completely insane with fear of this griz they had never actually seen. They were so anxious to get off the tundra; they were willing to leave all the equipment behind and jump into the plane with just their clothes on their backs. I managed to prevail upon them to clean up the mess and throw things into the plane. In hind sight, I should have done what they wished, then gone back later and grabbed their rifles and anything else I wanted, but my ethics would not allow me to leave junk out in the country like that, so all the stuff went back to town with them.

They had the silly idea they should not have to pay for the hunt, since they had not gotten what they had come for and had had to put up with being bothered by the griz. We just laughed at them of course, because when you book a hunt out on the tundra in arctic Alaska, griz just come with the plan, just like the weather.

On the subject of griz, I had another humorous experience which involved some griz meat and an Eskimo girl upriver that I visited on a regular basis. She and I would have a good roll in the hay whenever I got to her village and one day when I flew in, she surprised me. I figured to have a quick tumble and head on back to the plane and fly away, just like normal.

The young lady in question offered me some griz ribs off the drying rack out behind the cabin, so I said yes. Now these ribs were just air dried with no refrigeration or protection of any kind. It was summer time and flies were a factor around all the drying racks in the village. Now the norm would have been for her to just dump the ribs in front of me and leave me to fend for myself thereafter. On this occasion, she grabbed an ulu, an Eskimo knife, and proceeded to scrape the fly eggs off for me. This was an indication that she had begun to like me. We were no longer just bed warmers for each other.

You would think this was no big deal, but her brother would come down to town once in a while and get loaded up in the bar. Then he would take it into his head he should screw my white girl friend, an idea she did not go for. Since she would turn down his advances, he thought I wouldn't let her screw him, so he would decide the thing to do was to kill me. Every time he would get blasted in town, we would go through this nonsense. I think his idea was that if I got to do his sister, he should be allowed to do my girlfriend. I couldn't have cared less about her or who she did, but he seemed to blame me for her reluctance.

This crap of him killing me came to a head one winter night in the bar when a couple other fights were underway. I was watching two native women try to tear each other apart and the guy from upriver decided this was the time to attack me. I got caught unawares and got hurt, which pissed me off. We began to try to kill each other, just like the women were doing. Luckily for me, I soon had the upper hand because I was not as drunk as he was. As a person of European ancestry, I am much better able to handle my booze than an Eskimo. I learned just how physically tough these people are that night. By the time we were pulled apart, I had beaten that SOB more badly than any other person ever and he was still trying to kill me even then. Having a metal bar stool crashed over your head will usually settle your hash, but not if the head belongs to an Eskimo.

After that, when I saw him either upriver or in town, he treated me like were best friends and we never had to go for it again. As for his sister, she still liked me clear till I left the country. We shared many a good time over the years.

On another occasion of trying to get a native guy to calm down, I was on the ground in Point Hope, a little tiny village out on the end of a spit of land pointing toward the Soviet Union from extreme northwest Alaska. I saw a three wheeler coming toward my plane across the tundra as fast as the driver could get it to go. If his rig had had wings, he would have been flying it. He came screaming up to the plane, jumped off his rig and piled onboard. He was frantic for me to get in the air and take him to Kotzebue and did not care about anything else such as moving his rig out of the way. I was not in any great hurry and I asked him what was wrong. He frantically kept looking out the widow and saying for me to take him to Kotzebue.

We both saw another rig coming across the tundra and he freaked out. The other guy coming out was coming to kill him and he really was not interested in being killed by him. Of course I did not know this and waited for the other guy, thinking he wanted to go to town and I would get more money from him. When he jumped off his three -wheeler and piled into the plane, he attacked the guy in the back seat. This was not tolerable to me, so I threw him out of the plane. He tripped over the landing gear and fell on his ass. When he got up, he came right back into the plane and attacked the other guy again. I really did not care about the fight but I did care about my plane, so I threw him out again and again, he tripped over the gear and fell on his ass. The third time he tried it, I had my 357 revolver out and as he came through the door, I whacked him across the bridge of his nose with the handle as hard as I could swing it. This cooled his jets and he collapsed on the ground. I got out and dragged him and the two rigs out of the way and took off.

On the way down to town, I asked the guy in the back "who was that sumbitch?" He said "he is the mayor of Point Hope." Oh great. So of course I had to ask the owner to come out into the hanger when we got to town for a conversation.

I told my boss what had happened and what I had done. He asked me if I had killed the guy or just knocked him into the middle of next week. I told him I was pretty sure he was not dead. The owner just said "don't worry about it, no big deal." It never came up again.

Down in the village of Deering, on the north side of the Seward Peninsula, lived a girl with a special place in her heart for pilots. The deal was that she did not have the time of day for you unless you could show her a pilot's license. Well of course that was not a problem for me, so every time I got to her village and went to her place, her pants just fell right to the floor. When I would take the telephone guys down there, they wanted to know where I was going while they did their thing with the village phones, so I told them about this girl. One of the phone guys wanted to do her, so I introduced the two of them and, of course, she asked to see his license, which he did not have. She told him to get lost and that was that.

On the way back up to town after that trip, the phone guy pleaded with me to help him get somewhere with her. Largely as a joke, I suggested that the next time he went down to Anchorage; he should get with an FAA doctor and get a student pilot's certificate and third class medical certificate. He got all excited and asked if it would really work with her. I told him I had no idea if she would go for it, but at least he would have a piece of paper with the word pilot across the top. He thought he would need some kind of paper work to make it happen, but I said no, you don't need anything, just be prepared to write a check when it is over.

A couple months later, he saw me in the bar and was all excited to show me his new student pilot's certificate he had gotten down in Anchorage. I looked it over and said we could give it a try with the girl next time we went down to

Deering. It did not take him long to get a trip set up to go down there and request me as his pilot.

When we got to Deering, instead of going to do his telephone job, he wanted to go right over to this girl's house, so off we went. When she came to the door she told me to come right in and told him to get lost. He told her "I've got a pilot's license", and she asked to see it. He looked at me and pulled it out. She looked it over, smiled and said "come right in." So it worked for him just fine and he probably couldn't even spell airplane, let alone fly one, but she didn't know the difference.

Well, things just kind of purred along, flying and working all the time. My routine was to work six days a week and take Sunday off. This meant I flew a great deal. There was a point in there somewhere that I flew 175 hours in 30 days, something that today would be against the law, but it was legal then. We flew in all kinds of weather and conditions. We would have structural icing as a factor every single day of the year. There were times when the weather would be so terrible we would not be able to get in without special clearance from the Flight Service Station. This was always a problem because there was no fuel anywhere else we could reach, so we HAD to get in.

There came the inevitable day of horrible weather, ice fog and blowing snow with the visibility down to zero, varying to one mile, and I got the short straw for a mechanical problem with my plane. The temperature was down around 40 below and the rubber drive belt for the generator and vacuum pump could not take the strain, so it chose that day to let go in flight. Now this may not sound too serious, but without those two engine parts working, I lost the two most important flight instruments in front of me. I was now down to backup instruments in the worst winter storm you could ask for. The good news was that icing was not a factor that day. The bad news was I could not find the runway and my battery was not going to last very long at all in these conditions, with no generator to keep it going.

I called for weather and was told it was below landing minimums, so I just decided to head on in anyway because the idea of parking my plane out on the tundra at 40 below did not have a lot of appeal. I could not see the tundra to land on it anyway, so this really meant find the runway or die. In some circles, this would be an emergency, but among the few of us bush pilots still alive, this was just the way we got the job done. Like I said earlier, we made choices every day; get out, get killed, or get good. I survived.

These kinds of experiences tend to get a guy to thinking about what life might hold for me if I stay in this game much longer. I had many an opportunity to talk with the Alaska Airlines guys and go into their cockpits. Those nice warm jets with multi-engines that never failed sure looked good to me and so did the girls riding around in the back serving coffee. I had never forgotten my plan to drive those big jets some day. I loved the flying in the Arctic and I had fulfilled my goals of being a bush pilot and guide, but I knew there was a bigger world out there and I needed to go see more of it.

Somewhere in there, I fell ass end over tea kettle in love with a sweet little Eskimo girl and that kind of scared me. She was a beauty and I could easily have gotten tangled up in a marriage if I had not gotten my head out of my ass and had a cup of coffee. I took a realistic assessment of my situation and decided the thing to do was to head out, when I could get the money together, and finish my Bachelors degree so a real airline would at least give me an interview. Without a BS or BA in those days, a pilot did not stand a chance of getting in the door.

A guy that I knew well who mushed dogs was killed in a completely avoidable crash at about the same time and that really got to me. The pilot was from down in Nome and he did not know the country up where we were flying. He chose to take off into the worst icing storm we had had in a long time. None of the local guys were flying that day; we had called it quits and agreed to go to the bar. Every flight that did get in the air that morning had turned back because of the icing. Guys had told the Flight Service of the extreme icing and this info was available to the guys down in Nome, so the decision to try and make it to Ambler was a mistake. Well, as the flight got closer to our neck of the woods, the ice got worse and the pilot did not know the country as well as we did, so where the highest hill in the area is, he was too low. The hill won. They hit about 50 feet below the top and both the pilot and my friend the musher were killed on impact. The handler and several of the dog team went through the windshield. The handler broke numerous bones as she went through the window and hit the ground. All the dogs were badly injured or killed.

When the flight never made it to Ambler, a search was called, but due to the icing, no one could fly for several hours. When we could get in the air, it did not take long before we heard the emergency locator beacon on the emergency frequency and homed in on the crash. The Alaska air guard helicopter got in and found the dead guys and assumed they were the only ones on the plane. They saw dogs, both dead and wounded, all over the area. A crew member from the chopper went to try and help some of the hurt dogs and found the handler farther up the hill. She was still alive with several dogs around her. She would have died but for the dogs giving her their body heat. They were all badly hurt, yet out of loyalty to their handler; they had stayed with her and kept the cold and the wolves away.

The Alaska air guard guys got the handler and the still living dogs out along with the musher and the pilot. This was a completely avoidable accident and it could happen to any of us at any time. We had to make decisions every day and all we could do was hope they were the right ones every time. The decision to take off to Ambler that day was a mistake. The decision to continue once he entered the icing was a mistake. The decision to descend where he did was a mistake, although he may not have had a chance by then due to the icing. All in all, it was a tough day for all of us that knew the musher and his family.

A number of the villages in northwest Alaska were going through the charade of voting themselves dry at about this time. What this meant was that they would pass a village ordinance outlawing the sale, possession or importation of alcoholic beverages. So of course the consumption of Welch's grape juice and yeast went way up, because the Eskimos would pour the grape juice and the yeast in a fish tub and let it set for a couple days. This would turn into something they called wine and it would knock them on their asses, but it tasted more like sewer water or worse. The idea of cleaning out the fish tubs before they made the wine never occurred to them and the result was repulsive to me.

Along came the day I had a guy from up in Kivalina in my plane that I knew fairly well. We had fished and hunted together several times and he had shared his wife with me on a few occasions, so we were pretty good friends. Well, he outs with a bottle of booze from under his coat and takes a big drink of it. I told I would have to turn around now and go back to town because I could not allow him to take that booze into the village. He convinced me nothing would happen when we got there, so I continued to the village. As I expected, he told me to come to his house and have a go with his wife, so I put the engine cover on the plane and we went to the house.

When we got there, he told her to take care of me, said he would be back in a while, and walked out the door. We were just getting our pants back on when he came back and knocked on his own door to let us know he was there. He waited a few minutes, then came in with a big package in his arms. The package was wrapped up in old wrinkly brown paper which had obviously seen better days. He gave it to me and said "it is for you." I said "thank you, what is it?" He told me it was a gift for letting him bring in the bottle of booze. I unwrapped the package and found a complete skull and tusks of a bull walrus. At that time, and this was many years ago, that was worth thousands of dollars. He told me he had shot the walrus out on the ice and had lots of them so it was for me. To this day, I still have that as one of my most prized trophies from my hunting and collecting around the world. I do not know if he thought the bottle of booze was worth it, but I did.

One day I was weathered in in the village of Noatak, so I decided to go to the trading post and get warm until the weather lifted enough to get in the air. It happened that it was about lunch time and when I got inside, the owner was just about to lock up and go home for lunch. He invited me to go with him and on the way he asked me if I was married. I said "no, I've never been married, why do you ask?" He said "well, I've got six daughters looking for husbands". So I had a pretty good idea what I was going to be doing until the weather cleared up some.

When we got in the house, he made all the daughters do something for me, get a cup of coffee, hang up my down gear, help me with my boots, or whatever. They were all very nice to me and I to them. The father and I had lunch over the course of about an hour or so, with all the daughters in attendance. Each one of them had to do something to serve me, so my coffee cup was never empty and the caribou eyeball stew never seemed to end. The girls would cut some meat off the frozen trout and serve me what I now know is called sushi, but at the time it was just native food. The Eskimo diet is almost all meat and they do not waste anything edible, and I do mean anything.

So our lunch break was about over and it was time for dad to go back to the trading post, so, as expected, he asked me which daughter I wanted. In an effort to be diplomatic, and not wanting to offend anyone girl (remember, he had six daughters), I answered that I liked them all. He looked quite surprised at me and said "well, all right, you can have them all", and told the girls they were all to take care me. They did.

As planned, I was putting money away in the bank from my earnings every pay day. There came the magic day when I reached my goal in the bank and started making plans to get away from life with the Native peoples of the Arctic and head out to the lower 48. I did not have any way of knowing what the future held or where I would find myself in years to come, but I knew I could leave the north with my head held high. I had set myself the goal of becoming an Arctic bush pilot and hunting guide. I had done it. I had survived the most demanding flying environment on earth. I had made good at flying the bush where it is acknowledged to be the deadliest form of aviation, second only to combat helicopter flying, in terms of deaths. I had seen friends die in the same game. I had come to know and love the Eskimo people, I had earned their respect and trust, had been given the most intimate access to their lives that any outsider could ask for.

A Native guy had given me an Eskimo name and it stuck. The name was Natuck and it had two meanings, either a spirit or a snowy owl, depending on how it was used. This was gained on a hunt out on the ocean ice one day for oogruck, the bearded seal. We had gone out at first light onto the ice with no snow rigs, only walking, so as to make no noise. One of the hunters spotted a dark shape on the ice and we all moved silently around the seal, encircling him. The signal, a call of a sea gull, was given, and all the hunters shot for the head. This was to ensure the seal died instantly to prevent him from going under the ice, never to be seen again.

We all worked very hard for next several minutes to roll this 900 pound animal over on the ice and butcher him out. Then came the interesting part. As soon as we had him opened up, the native guys cut out the entire liver, which weighed about 40 or 50 pounds. The seal was not even dead 15 minutes and here we were eating the liver raw, still warm with the body heat. The idea was to put all you could into your mouth, while another guy cut it off in front of your lips with an ulu, an Eskimo knife. The liver was then passed to the next guy and the process continued until the entire liver was eaten.

After the hunt was over, I got my name because of the willingness I had shown to be just as much a man of the ice as they. I had earned the respect of a people who had in turn earned mine and leaving them was not easy. I was not to be deterred from my goal however and into the future I was going to go. So on that note, I left the Arctic and headed back south, to the lower 48.

Chapter Twelve

Upon arrival in Ellensburg, Washington for another go at Central Washington University, I immediately needed housing and soon found myself in a duplex off campus. I got an appointment with a college advisor whose job it was to separate me from my money as fast as possible. By that, I mean he wanted to sign me up for all kinds of bullshit classes I neither wanted nor needed. I approached this college endeavor with a plan. I told them when I was going to graduate, and then asked how to get to that date successfully. We went round and round with lots of needless wasted words and finally got to an understanding. The advisor went through the motions of telling me I could not do what I had set for myself as a goal, to which I said something like "watch me." I was, again, now several years older and a lot more worldly than most college juniors. Few, if any, of the students at CWU had ever even met an

Eskimo, let alone lived with them and made good as a bush pilot.

I now set out on the tedious path of being a college student again. I took education classes and aerospace sciences at the same time. My goal was to complete two majors and two years, junior and senior, in five quarters. There were times I wanted to not study, there were times I wanted to just split for the open spaces. I longed for the hoped for day I could return to my beloved Alaska, the wild country I missed so much. But I hung in there and put up with the rules of campus bullshit and the childish antics of the professors and the students. I had a goal and, just like the others in my life, I intended to see this thing through to the end.

I made some friends there and we went fishing a few times and got out into the field for a bit of hunting, but every day, I missed Alaska. The college girls were all so shallow and cute but they did not hold anything long term for me. Cute by itself did not do much for me and shallow was just annoying, but I had my share of fun in those days. The guys I befriended and I figured out that we were all working too hard for what we were after, because it just did not seem it should require so much effort to BS your way through school, and that is just what we did.

In the spring of my senior year, United Airlines had a pilot strike and I got invited to interview with them. The airline paid for the ticket to Denver and back and the lodging, so I went down to Denver and made a fool of myself in the interview and especially in the simulator check ride. I went, not even knowing there were such things as simulators and of course I blew it. In hind sight, had I succeeded, I would have been hired as a scab, a position I would not have liked, so it was best for me that they told me to get lost.

So I went back to college, dejected and rejected. The rest of my senior year did not really matter to me, I just went through the motions and sent off resumes, not really caring about the education, I just wanted to be through and gone. Then came that phone call from the north. "Dave," the caller said, "do you want to come back to Alaska and fly for us?" I had some floozy girl friend around at the time, but she did not matter at all when I said "hell yes."

So now the stage was set for me to return to the Great Land, a dream I had all but lost while buried in the minutiae of college. My agreement was that, upon graduation, I was to get to Anchorage as soon as possible and go to work flying twin otters, a plane I knew of but had never flown.

The graduation day came and I invited a bunch of people to come over to my rental house for a beer drinking contest to celebrate our graduation. My long suffering parents came over and of course disapproved of my friends and my drinking, but they were glad both of their sons were now college graduates. Everyone got blasted out of our skulls and my very good and long long term friend was there with his first wife. She got too smashed to function and decided to get in the car and drive who knows where. My friend had had the foresight to disable the car because apparently she liked to do stupid things when she got drunk and he had seen it coming. My rental house got destroyed by the party and people pissing in rooms other than the bathroom and all kinds of good things like that. Two days later, I took my brand new college degree and split for Alaska. Few things have made me happier than that day, getting gone from college and heading back to the land I missed and loved so much.

This time I would be living in Anchorage, not out in the bush where I had been before. The only Eskimos I would see now would be the drunks down on 4th Avenue. Bush or no bush, I was returning to Alaska and I could not have been happier.

Chapter Thirteen

When I met the chief pilot, he turned out to be a short ugly little dude who told me in no uncertain terms just how little he thought of the company and any pilot who worked for them any length of time. His statement was something like "any pilot who is still here after six months must be a fool." I had spent enough years in Alaska already to know what I was hearing, so I resolved to be gone soon.

The chief pilot and I went out for a flight in the twin otter and he seemed to like the way I flew. I had been hired over the phone and could of course be fired on the spot. It was therefore incumbent upon me to fly well or be told to hit the bricks. Since I had no other options, just like in the Arctic, it was fly or die. So I flew.

The name of the company was Alaska Aeronautical Industries, or AAI. The standing joke among the customers and the pilots was that the letters stood for Ask About Insurance. We primarily flew down to Homer, Kenai and Kodiak from Anchorage. One of the humorous things I encountered while there was the opinion among the new pilots from Outside was that they were bush pilots. I, as a real bush pilot, just had to laugh at their naiveté. They had no idea of the reality of being a bush pilot. All these beginners were was pilots flying in Alaska, not bush pilots. They never had a clue.

One day, a bright spot came in the door. An old buddy from the bush showed up on the property, a man I truly treasured the friendship of. This would be a man I had flown with in the toughest weather the world could throw at us. He and I had a bond that distance, time and separation could not dim. We had shared lodging, airplanes, women, booze, good times and bad, poker games, fishing and hunting, you name it we had done it together. So it is safe to say we were good friends. So when we got past the handshakes and "how are you" sessions, I was a little surprised when he said no to having a beer after work.

It turned out that my best male friend I have ever had was not the same guy I had come to know in the bush. It turned out that while I was off in the lower 48 getting an education, He had met a white girl in the north and had fallen in love! This was not something we pilots were supposed to do. As if this were not enough, he had up and married her. Our after work beer turned out to be my meeting the girl he had fallen for and I liked her right away. I do not think she liked me very well because she thought she had gotten her husband away from the bush mentality and now here was Dave, leading her husband back down that road.

We talked all through how we had come to be in Anchorage together and where we thought things were going from here. My friend and I had played on the pilot's baseball team together up north and while I was down south getting educated, he had moved down to Nome and started flying for an outfit down there. This was where he had come across this girl. They had hit it off and now they were married. She was a transplant from down in Minnesota and seemed to like the North Country alright. Just how the two of them had met never did come clear. It probably had something to do with the beer. My lack of understanding that is.

My friend and I had our share of flying with AAI, and, like a lot of relationships in my life, the one with AAI ended. Another old bush pilot buddy of mine had called me and said "why don't you get on with Mark Air?" I immediately applied to them and nothing happened. One day, it seems like it was a Friday; I called them up and asked what was going on with my application. The woman who answered the phone asked what I was doing that afternoon. I told her I was free and she said "why don't you come in today for an interview?" Thus I went to AAI on Monday morning and told them to take this job and shove it, or something like that.

Leaving AAI to go be a Flight Engineer on a 4 engine Lockheed Hercules was a huge step in my career. Just going from single engine planes to twin otters had been a big deal to me, now here I was going to truly big airplanes. Yes I was intimidated. I had no reason to think I could do this, but I sure as hell wasn't going to back down from a challenge. I talked it over with my friend and he thought it was a good move.

For the first time in my career, I was actually hired by an airline to be a crewmember. Yes, I was only the engineer, but for those of you that know, this was the entry level position for an airline cockpit in those days. The training consisted of an actual classroom, not just getting in an airplane and fly. This was something new to me. I had books to read, tests to take, things to memorize. At the end of the training, I had a long oral exam to pass with the FAA for the Flight Engineer Turbo Prop rating, a test I had to pass or be out on the street, along with the practical test. These things came after the written, which I had already passed as a prerequisite for the job.

My efforts had the desired outcome and I went out on the line as an FE. I had to fly with senior guys for a while, who watched me do my thing and then they said I was graduated to go fly around on my own. This was the beginning of my life in big airplanes for awhile. Our routine was to fly all over the state of Alaska, to such garden spots as Deadhorse, Barrow, Nome, Unalakleet, Kotzebue, Coldfoot, Prudhoe Bay, and lots of other places no one in the lower 48 ever heard of. I was now in a position to go see all the other places in Alaska I could not have seen in single engine planes. We flew a lot.

There came the day I got called to work from my apartment in the afternoon after I had been awake for most of the day already. The trip was to go up to the slope and back, be gone about 12 to 14 hours, no big deal. From the time I got aboard the plane until I got off turned out to be over 40 hours continuously on the airplane. By the time I got back to my apartment in Anchorage, I had been awake almost 60 hours. So when pansy asses start talking to me about being tired or sleep deprived, I either don't give a shit or don't care, depending on whether it is my mother or not. As a seasoned international airline pilot, I probably know more about sleep deprivation than anyone not in my work.

Then of course came the night I suddenly realized this Flight Engineer business was not for me. It was about 55 below zero with a nice breeze blowing off of Siberia onto the northwest corner of Alaska, and the pilots had gone into the warm-up shack, leaving me out at the plane to do my FE duties. One of those duties was to get up on the wings and check the prop fluid in all four engines. This was not fun at 55 below in the wind. The idea of being blown off the wing and busting my ass on the ice below just did not have a lot of appeal. So there I sat on engine #3, pouring prop fluid into the hub, and I happened to look over at the warm-up shack to see the two pilots sitting in there in their shirt sleeves drinking coffee.

After getting off the wings, I had other things to do, including going in to tell the other guys it was time to leave. I could think of a few other things I wanted to say, but it would not have done any good. I was the junior guy on the crew. I have always believed the best course is to call a spade a spade, but this was one of those times it was best to refer to a spade as a shovel. (This is one of the gems of wisdom I got from my father, a good man.) So I bit my tongue and, for once, did something smart and kept my mouth shut.

Things rolled along with Mark Air, and soon enough I was asked if I wanted to go to co-pilot school. I did not have to think twice and so was soon on my way to the right seat instead of the engineer's seat. This involved a few trips down to a place I, like every Alaskan, was very prejudiced against. It is called California. There used to be a base there called El Toro Marine Air station and they had a simulator for the Hercules. We would fly down on Western Airlines, do a weekend in the simulator when the Marines were not there, then fly back to Anchorage and go back to work as an Engineer.

Eventually, I got through co-pilot school and was designated a First Officer with Mark Air on the Hercules, a four engine turbo prop plane widely flown around the world by a lot of Air Forces. At the time, Mark Air was one of a very few airlines using this plane in civilian operations as a freighter. Thus it was that I became an official Freight Dog, a title those of us who have worn it wear proudly. I know all you guys out there who think you are hot shit because you fly people haulers don't want to hear it, but we freight dogs are not ashamed of what we do.

Being a First Officer on the Hercules was a big step up career-wise and I was glad to have made the change. I no longer had to crawl around under the plane in the snow to check the brakes and other good things like that. I no longer had to climb up onto the wings in a blizzard and check the prop fluid. I was now the pilot sitting in the warm up shack drinking coffee.

Shortly after all the checks and tests to become an FO, I heard about a trip to go outside the state of Alaska. I thought that was pretty cool and asked about it. I was told that "yes, there is a trip Outside, would you like to be on that crew?" Of course I said yes and so I had my first trip to the Lower 48 as a working crewmember. We flew a plane down to a field in Michigan called Willow Run Airport and started flying from there, hauling auto parts to assembly plants all over the Lower 48. It worked pretty well for the pilots because the company put us up in a nice hotel in Anne Arbor and we did alright for our selves. We flew almost every day or night as the case may be and I learned a lot of things about flying as a crewmember instead of as a single pilot. Being part of a crew instead of a single pilot in a single engine plane is much safer. Having four big engines with unlimited power was pretty nice too. An engine failure in that Hercules was almost a nonevent, as opposed to an engine failure in a single engine bird.

We got the word from the company that we were to fly down to Miami and go to the hotel to await further developments. That is what we did and while there I had a rather humorous phone call one night. Remember, this was before the days of cell phones.

I was sound asleep when the phone rang. I answered it and heard the familiar hiss and hum of a long distance call. The voice on the other end said "where are you?" I answered "in bed" and hung up. I did not know who it was and had been dead to the world, so my reaction was probably not the wisest. Of course the phone soon rang again and now I was a little more awake. When I answered, the caller again said "where are you." This time I asked "where did you call?" The caller answered "the Miami Hilton." I said "that is probably where I am." It turned out to be crew scheduling and they just wanted to BS and make sure we were where we supposed to be.

The trip we were standing by for did not ever happen, but it had been planned and then never executed. The destination was Nicaragua, which would have been my first international flight.

That first international flight was not too far off for me. We headed back up to Alaska and did a crew rotation. While in Anchorage on days off, I went to the office and talked about the operation down in Michigan with crew scheduling. I understood that most of the guys did not want to go out of Alaska for extended times for all kinds of reasons. I had no one I cared about, so it worked for me to go and stay outside with the plane. I made them an offer that, if accepted, would scratch both their back and mine. I said that if they would promise to keep me out, I would promise to stay out. Of course they jumped on that offer, and the deal was made. I parked my car in a friend's yard and got out of my apartment, so I had no phone, no address, no insurance bills and no strings attached to me. The company would cover my expenses and lodging and I had no over head, so I could put some real money in the bank.

Then came my first international trip. We got called in the hotel to get ready to head to Iceland. America had a president in those days named Ronald Reagan and the Soviet Union had a guy named Gorbachov at its head. These two leaders had agreed to meet in Iceland for a conversation. There was a new company around called CNN and we had been contracted to fly the equipment out to Iceland so the whole world could see and hear these two leaders and the results of their meeting. We had to have the equipment there before the meeting and then stay till after it was over to bring it back. This resulted in my going to Iceland for a week.

The things we had to do to find our way from the USA out to Iceland and back were all new to me then and I loved it. Since I had never done it before and had never gotten any training in how to do long distance oceanic navigation, that poor Captain had his hands full. I respect and admire him to this day. He basically was doing it all alone and trying to teach the things to me I did not know at the same time. We made it.

Iceland turned out to be a beautiful country with lots of very good looking women that seemed to be quite friendly towards us. All the guys in the crew had a good time. We were stunned at the price of booze there and after the first bar tab, we all became non drinkers until we got back to the USA.

We went back to Michigan and flew auto parts for a while, until the next trip overseas came up. My second one was to the lovely nation of Ireland. We landed in Shannon and this time my ocean crossing was not a classroom because I now had some clue what to do and how to do it. Like virtually all first time visitors to Shannon, Ireland, I went to a place called Dirty Nellie's. There I met a very pleasant

Irish lass who really liked Yankees, or at least she really liked this one for a day and a night.

I had found a new niche for myself. If the world of international flying was this much fun, I would have it. Ocean crossings were a little intimidating at first, but, like all the flying I had done before, I soon had this mastered.

I had gotten very accustomed to this position of First Officer and thus was quite shocked to be told I was going to have an Engineer's check ride when I got back to Alaska. Shock or no shock, an FE is what I now went back to being. While I had been out of Alaska for all those months, the price of oil got down to $10 a barrel. In the state of Alaska, this was not good news. The company had furloughed a bunch of pilots under me on the seniority list and I had slid backward into the FE position again.

Right after that rude shock, we took off for the North Pole. We flew from Anchorage to the magnetic north pole in the Canadian Arctic. We went to an oil camp right on top of the magnetic pole and flew from there to remote drill sights out on the ice on top of the world to bring the exploration rigs in off the ice. This involved another variety of navigation called grid navigation. This is because the compasses in the plane do not know where to point, so I had to learn about this. I was not a pilot now, but it was fascinating to observe from the FE chair.

Polar bears were a common sight in and around the camp. The camp had a pack of big, long-haired dogs whose job it was to bark at the bears so we people could get into a building for protection when we heard the dogs. Men sometimes lose their minds in the extreme isolation and loneliness which is part and parcel of being on the top of the world. As a result, there are no firearms in camp, for fear of a guy going nuts and shooting up the place. There also were no women, as that prevented guys from fighting over jealousy or attentions or whatever, and lastly, there was no alcohol. So our only protection from the polar bears was to get into a building or an airplane.

A bunch of us were in the mess hall killing time when we heard the dogs start going crazy. One of the guys at a window called out that the bear was about to catch a dog and so we all went to the window to watch. The unfortunate dog seemed to realize he was done for and ran to the mess hall and threw himself against the door in a vain attempt to get inside. Had he kept running instead of letting the bear corner him, he probably would have gotten away, but that was a mistake which cost him his life. The bear caught and killed him right outside the window just a few feet from us. Of course there was nothing we could have done to help the dog. A polar bear is not something you go hit with a broom or something.

After spending a couple weeks out on the ice at the North Pole closing down camps, it was time to head back to Anchorage. Almost as soon as we got back, I was asked if I would go on a classified mission for which there was no more info. It was yes or no time, so of course, I said yes. Off I went to the lower 48 to pick up the plane in Michigan. We then flew across the pond to Egypt, which is a very long trip in a Hercules. This oceanic navigation was becoming old hat.

Well, in Egypt, things do not always work the way they do in Europe or the USA. As FE, it was my job to fuel the plane and that meant trucks of fuel coming out to where we were. As luck would have it, I wanted fuel during prayer time. When the first truck ran out of fuel, the guy driving it told me it would be about 30 minutes to an hour before the next one came, and he made it clear that was Egyptian time, not my time. I invited this character up into the cockpit for a visit. On the back of the cockpit wall was a frontal nude fold out picture of a very beautiful and voluptuous woman.

This poor Egyptian guy did not know what to think say or do. He reached out to touch it as though he would get a burned finger. I told him was OK, go ahead. When he did actually touch the picture and Allah did not strike him dead, he started jabbering excitedly in Arabic and of course I could not understand him. I told him he could have a whole magazine of pictures like that if he would just get me some fuel.

That offer set off a bunch of excited radio chatter which soon resulted in three fuel trucks in a race out to my plane. The drivers did not give a damn about the fuel; they all wanted to see that picture. I got my fuel and each driver got a magazine.

Shortly after getting back to Alaska, I saw a copy of the current seniority list, and my name was at the bottom of it. It did not take a rocket scientist to figure out what was coming next. My old buddy from the bush had already lost his job in Alaska and, like thousands of other Alaskans, he had had to leave the state to find work. He had gone to that much despised place called California and gotten on flying down there. Cheap oil was great for everyone else, but it was terrible for those of us who called Alaska home at the time.

I called up my old friend and said I needed a job yesterday, how are things down in California? He told me to come on down, he could get me on right away. So I left that big beautiful state to the far north, to head for the hated California. I vowed I would return in a maximum of one year. How that fickle finger of fate fingers us sometimes.

Chapter Fourteen

I showed up for the interview with the outfit where my old friend was working and was very disillusioned by what I saw and heard. At the end of the interview, I was told some line of crap about how they would call me in a week or so. Of course I needed a job; I had nothing, so I went to an interview with American Eagle, figuring that the gig with United Express was not going to pan out. The people I met at American Eagle were much more professional and organized. They asked more intelligent questions and did not fool around with this crap of letting me know sometime next week. They just hired me to fly better airplanes at $5 an hour more than the other guys were offering. The decision was not hard to make. So when the other outfit called to tell me they were not interested in me, I just said the feeling is mutual and hung up the phone.

I was holed up with my old friend and his wife out in some little town in central California called Riverbank. It was a huge relief to be able to tell him I had gained employment in just two days of trying. He had been true to his word, I had gotten on, but it was not the outfit he was with.

American Eagle did real training in a classroom and books and all that. A new pilot had to apply himself to learn this new airplane and new company. Californians do not do things like Alaskans, so I had a lot to learn in a hurry. In Alaska, when a man says he is going to do something, he is going to do it. It is a thing called honor. To an Alaskan, your word is your bond and a handshake means an agreement has been reached. To a Californian, honor has no meaning and your word is just hot air. Lying and deceiving are considered art forms to most of the Californians I met in those first days in the state. So it is safe to say I was not very socially comfortable for a while.

The training got finished up and I went to the line in San Francisco as a new hire co-pilot or First Officer. The first couple days in the San Francisco area were real eye openers for me. In the freight dog world from which I came, there were no women to speak of, and now every place I turned I was seeing good looking women. All the gate agents were young women, all the ticket agents, most of the ground employees were women. I began to think maybe this hated place California had some merits after all.

I got to know a guy who was senior to me and had a house up in Vallejo, north of San Francisco. He offered to let me stay with him for a price. Things were a little rough soon and I stayed only about two months. While there, I found a Chinese girl who liked to come over and warm the bed a bit and then go to work. She would often come by after work as well so I thought that worked pretty well. She reminded me of all the Eskimos I had shared good times with up north. Well she was married to some guy and, sure enough, he showed up one afternoon and told her it was time to go home. She just got up and followed him out the door without a word to me and I never saw her again.

Some of the privileges of being a working pilot include the jump seat privilege, which means that we pilots can ride for free in the cockpits of other carrier's planes. On one of my forays with another company, I met a very stunningly beautiful flight attendant, with the old airline Pacific Southwest Airlines, or PSA. She and I hit it off and started seeing each other all the time. Because we both worked for an airline, we could travel all over the place and get together a lot. For the first time in my working life, I think I was starting to feel something for a white girl besides lust. I had begun to actually care. So when the day came that a PSA employee went to work with a firearm and got into the cockpit in flight and shot the pilots, I was concerned because I knew she was scheduled to be flying at that time. I went down to the PSA operations office and asked if she was on that flight. The ops guy was very nervous and would not give me a straight answer. He kept saying "I can't say, I can't say," but he kept trying to get me to look down. There was a list of employee names and hers was on it. My beautiful flight attendant was dead. There had been no survivors.

About a month after losing her, I was asked if I wanted to go to Captain's school. I accepted. On one more trip as an FO, I met a new flight attendant from United Airlines. She and I hit it off very well the first time we met and so began my next exciting adventure. Off I went to training for captain school and my new girlfriend, who could fly anywhere for free, showed up at school with me on her days off. We partied so much and so hard, I don't know how I made it through, but I did. Graduation consisted of a check ride with the company check airman after passing numerous oral and written tests. This was not like being a bush pilot. I had to actually work at it and the cost of failure was high. My new girlfriend did not help at all, but we had a lot of fun.

I was now a newly minted commuter pilot Captain and was flying from San Francisco to all kinds of airports in California and southern Oregon. The weather was always good and there was little in the way of challenges or excitement to make it interesting and I was soon bored out of my mind. There just wasn't the aura of fun and exciting flying I had been doing up north. My flight attendant girl friend and I got together in lots of places and had a lot of fun together, but it did not last very long. She told me over the phone she had had enough and that was that. So one more time I was looking for something I had not yet found and did not even know what it was. I think I had glimpsed it with my girl friend from PSA, but she was dead.

My old buddy and his gracious wife were my steadfast friends in California, otherwise I hated the place. Too many people and too many rules and no honorable people summed up my view of California. Only an old Alaskan buddy kept me from going nuts. I wound up living in a flop house with about six other people and a nutty old Jehovah's Witness in Daly City, a community just south of San Francisco. One of the residents was a crazy queer who never missed a chance to bug me. The nutty old JW would harass me about the bible and I just went to work and flew trips to get away. Then one day something of interest came along. A memo came out from the chief pilot's office saying something like captains that were interested could go on temporary duty to Nashville to get a new American Eagle operation up and running. Of course I jumped on that. This resulted in my going to Nashville for about six months to fly around to

Ohio, Alabama, Mississippi, and numerous other places. Of course I soon met a girl in Nashville and off we went on a wild and crazy relationship consisting of a lot of drinking and sex and good times.

Her parents were farmers and very nice people up north of Nashville. She and I agreed to go up to go to church with them one Sunday morning after a heavy night of drinking and fun. The impression their daughter's new boyfriend made that morning in church probably wasn't too great.

After my tour in Nashville ended, I took my Tennessee girl friend out to California for her first time. She had never been out to the west before and this turned out to be quite a trip for both of us. We went all over the west and saw a lot of cool places and drank a huge amount of beer. But, like all good things, this too came to an end. The one thing I could say about it was that she and I had a good time. We went to places I had never been and I started to think maybe California was not so bad after all. It turns out there are a lot of mountains and pretty places there and for the first time I met some real people. Not the pompous, self centered, empty souled, shallow shits the place is famous for, but rather some decent, honorable, real people.

Like all the relationships that had gone before, my Tennessee girlfriend and I soon said goodbye to each other. It was not a big thing, she just moved on. The girls that like pilots tend to do that when they find out we aren't going to be around every night. It is never personal; they just want guys in their beds that will be there every night, not just when they happen to be in town.

Of course I was bored. My old friend from the bush and his wonderful wife were my rock of sanity in this place called California. I needed some sanity and they were the answer, though I doubt they knew it. I did not know any other Alaskans in the state. So one day when I saw a Hercules parked on the ramp at Sacramento International, it goes without saying I walked on over and talked to the Captain. He invited me up into the cockpit for a talk. I told him I had flown them up in Alaska and really liked the plane. He asked me a few questions and I told him the true answers. After a glance at my watch, I told him I had to go and he handed me his business card, Saying something like "if you think you ever want a job, give me a call." As I walked on back over to my plane, I glanced at the card. He turned out to be the west coast chief pilot for Southern Air Transport, the private airline of the Central Intelligence Agency. Now this was very fortuitous, as they were flying all over the world and I missed the international scene. Well, it did not take me long to figure out how to get my resume into his hands and that is what I did.

Time drifted by and I got a medical problem going which lead me to going to a hospital. Now at the time I did not know how else to see a doctor, so that is what I did. The person on the phone told me if I came to the emergency room I could see a doctor that day. I told her that my problem did not meet the level of emergency, but if that was how they did it in California, that is what I would do. She said to come on in, so to the hospital I went. I still had not gotten the hang of this California attitude.

My medical problem was soon cured and I thought no more about it until a month had gone by and I got a bill. I had taken care of my money issues, I thought, when I was at the hospital. This thing called insurance was supposed to take care of it and I had given the girl all the BS to take care of the money. Now here I was with a bill in my hands I should not have had. I called the hospital and got some syrupy voiced airhead on the phone. She took down all the info I had already provided at the initial visit and told me goodbye. In my opinion, I would hear no more from them. Wrong answer.

A month later I got another bill. They wanted the entire amount for the emergency room visit. I called them back and got the same syrupy voiced air head on the phone. She took down all the same info as before, assured me all was well and said goodbye. I assumed it was resolved and would hear no more from them. Wrong answer.

A month later I got another bill. They wanted the entire amount for the emergency room visit. I called them back and got the same syrupy voiced air head on the phone. She took down all the same info as before, assured me all was well and said goodbye. I assumed it was resolved and would hear no more from them. Wrong answer.

A month later I got another bill. You have the picture by now. This crap went on for four months, with me providing everything I was asked for and them not doing anything with it. It culminated in my receiving a notice that if I did not pay the full amount in 48 hours, it would go to a collection agency. This pissed me off. Now I am a patient guy, but enough is enough.

I called them back yet again and got the same syrupy voiced airhead on the phone. This time, when she offered to take down my info and take care of the problem, I said "no, I am sick of talking to you; I want to talk to someone with some brains." She said "yes sir, one moment," and put me on hold. The next voice I heard said "patient accounting, this is Olivia, may I help you?" I angrily told this new woman about my issues with her organization, and she listened carefully, asking intelligent questions and obviously making a real effort to help me. She asked me for a contact number and I gave it to her. A couple of hours later, she called me back and said "I have found your problem, it is taken care of, and I don't think you will hear from us again."

As a transplanted Alaskan, I needed to express my gratitude, since that is what we do, rather than just grunt stupidly. In my awkward, Alaskan way, I said" I really appreciate that; you ought to let me buy you a drink or something." She surprised me by saying "that sounds interesting." Well, I had put the offer out there and now it was time to pay the piper, so to speak. We agreed as to a time and place to meet and I was there. We went to what was then my favorite watering hole in San Francisco, a place called Irelands 32 Club. We had a few drinks together and then I looked at my watch. Noticing it was about dinner time, I asked her if she would like to have dinner with me. She said yes, and I have been buying her drinks and dinner ever since. That is how I met my wife of over 20 years, and I still like her

About the Author

The author has lived a life which is the stuff of dreams for many years. In this book he details the highs and lows of a very exciting career of flying for a living—few have done and fewer still have lived to write about. He is still an active international airline pilot.

Lightning Source UK Ltd.
Milton Keynes UK
UKHW042248041222
413345UK00002B/450

9 781452 083988